interview
with a grandmaster

by Aaron & Claire Summerscale

Everyman Publishers plc   www.everyman.uk.com

First published in 2001 by Everyman Publishers plc, formerly Cadogan Books plc, Gloucester Mansions, 140A Shaftesbury Avenue, London WC2H 8HD

British Library Cataloguing-in-Publication Data
A catalogue record for this book is available from the British Library.

ISBN 1 85744 243 1

Distributed in North America by The Globe Pequot Press, P.O Box 480, 246 Goose Lane, Guilford, CT 06437-0480.

All other sales enquiries should be directed to Everyman Chess, Gloucester Mansions, 140A Shaftesbury Avenue, London WC2H 8HD
tel: 020 7539 7600 fax: 020 7379 4060
email: dan@everyman.uk.com
website: www.everyman.uk.com

EVERYMAN CHESS SERIES (formerly Cadogan Chess)
Chief advisor: Garry Kasparov
Commissioning editor: Byron Jacobs

Typeset and edited by First Rank Publishing, Brighton.
Production by Book Production Services.
Printed and bound in Great Britain by The Cromwell Press Ltd., Trowbridge, Wiltshire.

CONTENTS

BIBLIOGRAPHY

Books

Attack with Julian Hodgson 1, Julian Hodgson (Hodgson Enterprises 1996)
Attack with Julian Hodgson 2, Julian Hodgson (Hodgson Enterprises 1997)
Chess in the Fast Lane, Bill & Michael Adams (Cadogan Books 1996)
Development of a Grandmaster, Bill & Michael Adams (Pergamon Chess 1991)
Easy Guide to the Ruy Lopez, John Emms (Everyman Chess 1999)
Meet the Masters, Cathy Forbes
The Inner Game, Dominic Lawson (Macmillan 1993)
The Najdorf Variation, Y Geller (RHM Press 1981)
The Polgar Sisters, Cathy Forbes (Batsford 1992)
The Taimanov Sicilian, Graham Burgess (Gambit 2000)
Understanding Chess Move by Move, John Nunn (Gambit 2001)
Winning Chess Brilliancies, Yasser Seirawan (Microsoft Press 1995)

Newspapers and Magazines

Chess Life, Chessbase Magazine, Melbourne Herald Sun, San Jose Mercury News, The Scotsman, New in Chess

Websites

Brainsturgeon.com, Chessbase.com, Chesscenter.com, Chessclub.com, Chess-mate.com, Chessnews.org, chessvariants.com, Clubkasparov.com, Concentric.net, Dromo.com, Dspace.dial.pipex.com, FIDE.com, Gmchess.com, Gmsquare.com, Hoogeveen.nl, Info.Exeter.ac.uk, Jlevitt.dircon.co.uk, kasparovchess.com, Lasvegassun.com, Members.iglou.com, Msoworld.com, Russiajournal.com, Thetimes.co.uk, Tiviakov.demon.nl, Uzweb.uz.ac.zw

INTRODUCTION

I was extremely nervous when I began to write this, my first book, until I realised that it actually had absolutely nothing to do with me. The fact is that this book is about two very specific sets of people: Grandmasters, without whose co-operation and words of wisdom this would be a very short book and, secondly, you – the players. You are the people who follow Grandmaster games and aspire, if not to play like them, certainly to play better chess.

This book has demanded lengthy research, using many different sources. In this technological age the Internet now presents us with an amazing wealth of information and I've spent hours (when I should have been looking at facts and numbers) reading through reams of endlessly entertaining and well-observed chess literature. Here, for example, is one rather poignant excerpt that I felt I should share with you:

'The Post Mortem: Many players specialise in this. Many's the time I've swaggered into the congress room set aside for this sort of thing with a defeated opponent (obviously I win all the time), only for said opponent to demonstrate conclusively how unbelievably lucky I was. How they missed fourteen wins in the first six moves alone, and how I managed to make a decent move on occasion only through a combination of blind luck and Faustian chicanery.

The Over-the-Shoulder Comment: You know who you are. These people pass by your Post Mortem, glance fleetingly at the board and then say something like 'Why didn't you do this? That wins the Queen' or 'Oh, you missed a mate in five there.' Aargh! Even if these suggestions are right, you are implying that in the past few seconds you have seen more deeply into the game than I have, despite sweating over it for four rotten hours, and unless your name begins with K and ends in V that is not the case!...' – Mark Blackmore.

I have certainly gone through these emotions, as I suspect a large number of you will have, but back to my research.

Many of you will have noticed me stalking the tournament halls, notebook in hand, pouncing on unsuspecting players and asking exactly what information they would like me to wrest from the Grandmasters. You had some very interesting questions to ask on a wide range of topics, but I would especially like to thank the player graded 82 BCF who, in response to my question 'what would you like to ask a Grandmaster?', replied in all seriousness that 'there was nothing that anyone could tell him, as he already knew everything', for making me laugh for days. None of us is close to knowing everything about chess. The richness of the game is to be found in its infinite variety, ever expanding variations and constantly changing theory.

It has been estimated that there are up to 500 million chess players in the world today, of which 565 are Grandmasters and 102 are Women Grandmasters. (Strangely, five of these hold the mysterious title of honorary Grandmaster). Grandmasters are not as widely acclaimed and certainly do not receive the same financial rewards as Premiership football players or basketball players, for example, yet they, too, are at the very top of their field of expertise. The admiration that they do receive is from players such as ourselves. We recognise their skill, their powers of calculation, their utter command over all sixty-four squares. But is it our fate to only dream of playing such chess?

Playing Grandmaster chess was certainly my dream from the moment that I saw my first chess set. I was convinced that I would plough my way unrelentingly through legions of players, win the British Championship with an extraordinary and never to be matched tally of 11/11, become Britain's greatest ever Grandmaster and then, without question, demolish whoever was the current World Champion! I'm sad to report that my dream still lies unrealised, but does this have to be the end of my Grandmaster ambition? As recently as August 2001 a team of German scientists produced a study that claims Grandmasters do not have different brains from us lesser players, they simply use a different part of their brain to calculate during play.

'Amateurs work by analysing new moves, trying to work out logically what their opponent's strategy is and how to counteract it. Experts simply delve into their memory banks of thousands of chess moves and pluck out the solution they need. A Grandmaster studies and practices for at least ten years to learn more than 100,000 patterns (memory chunks).' – Nigel Hawkes, *The Times*.

If pattern recognition is, therefore, the key, there may be hope for me yet, although I'm not entirely sure how I can program myself with 100,000 different chess scenarios without doing much work (did I fail to mention my slight laziness problem?). But this cannot be the solution to the mystery of the Grandmaster mind, can it? Where does talent and natural ability come into it? At present, we do not know their secrets – otherwise we too would be knocking on FIDE's door demanding our titles – but I intend to unlock them, perhaps not all at once, but piece by piece. Let me take you on a journey through the Grandmaster mind!

Claire Summerscale
London, November 2001

CHAPTER ONE

Michael Adams

Michael (Mickey) Adams' meteoric rise to fame was assured from the moment he picked up his first chess piece. At every stage of his chess career he seems to have set new records. He was the first player to win the British Under-11 title with a perfect 100% score, the third youngest player (behind Fischer and Kasparov) to achieve a Grandmaster norm and the third youngest player to obtain the Grandmaster title. Not content with these accomplishments, just one month later (August 1989) Mickey put his new Grandmaster title to good use, at the age of seventeen becoming the youngest ever British Champion.

1991 saw him conquer new heights when he became the first player to score the maximum 200/200 in the British Grand Prix and also saw his Elo rating break 2600 for the first time. Although 2600 is certainly not to be scoffed at, he has now left this level far behind, being ranked fourth in the world with a rating well over 2700.

Tell me about your chess playing background? How and when did your chess career begin?
I was about six or seven when I started but I don't remember too much until I was playing at school and in tournaments. I won my first tournament, so I suppose that wasn't too bad to start with. I won the Cornwall under-8 and under-10 titles when I was seven (I won them both; they were joint tournaments) so I guess I was pretty good then. I was quite into chess.

What is your earliest chess memory?
I definitely remember that tournament, and playing in school matches and so on around that time. The thing that I remember most is stalemating someone in a King's Gambit. I thought that I had some kind of mate after sacrificing my queen and it didn't actually work, so I sort of took all his pieces instead. I was rooks and pawns and a queen up and I stalemated him, so it was an eventful game!

How much truth is there to the well-established story that you managed to reach an extremely high level without working too hard?

I think that I was pretty lucky. I reached a good level without doing too much work but, at some stage, you're always going to hit a level that you can't really improve on without work. I found that level and had a few years where I didn't work too much and didn't really get anywhere. I think that in the past five or six years I've put a lot more work in and I've progressed, but I certainly managed to get to 2600+ pretty quickly without doing too much work, so that was pretty good.

'If you work harder for something you enjoy it more' – Michael Adams, New In Chess *1999.*

Was that because you have the amazing ability to 'sense' exactly where your pieces should be? Is this a skill that you're born with or is it something that people can learn?

I think that you definitely have to have some sort of talent and, obviously, somehow I did have that talent. I think that I've always been a good practical player as well, very good at turning in good performances in games and being tough when things don't go my way. A good temperament, that's one of the things that's worked for me.

What do you consider to be your greatest achievement and where do you see your ambitions leading you?

I've been pleased with the kind of rankings I've had, you know, 2700+ on several rating lists. Also my performances in World Championships, both in Professional Chess Association (PCA) and World Chess Federation (FIDE) events. I've normally done pretty well and been in the late stages of all of those. Basically, I've done well in the big events. That's what I aim to do really. I'm just carrying on, trying to improve and do as well as I can and seeing what happens. The chess world is in a state of flux at the moment. It's difficult to know what's going to happen. My immediate ambition would be the FIDE World Championships in Moscow, which should be in a couple of months, if all goes according to plan.

How do you prepare for the monster tournament that is the World Championship?

Normally I like to play a few games before, because it's a very quick format and you can be eliminated after a couple of days. I'll be playing in the European Teams in Leon and that will be quite useful, especially because it's with the same time limit, which I don't have any experience with at all yet, so that's going to be a bit of a problem this time. In general, you just have to be very well prepared because it's very hard to say who you are going to play, what openings you will get. It's really a test of your general strength and your overall level of preparation, as there's no way to focus on one particular opponent – the pairings aren't even out yet and the knockout possibilities quickly start to multiply.

Do you consider it to be an effective format or do you prefer the old cycles?
Well, I think that it's not a bad format because the zonals and interzonals were really not the kind of tournaments that you wanted to be involved in and they were terrible from a spectators' point of view, as there was always a large number of draws towards the end. And the continental championships I think have a similar problem, it's not really a good format and this bit you want to minimise as much as possible. I think that a knockout isn't bad, but I think the new time control is a big mistake, while playing tie-breaks on the second day instead of having a third day available just makes the tournament more random, which makes no sense. If you want to make it as good a tournament as possible, and since the players are paying for their accommodation, it's not really clear why they need to do this.

As for the new time control, there is no advantage really. I actually think that the Fischer clock has a lot to answer for, in that before it came along time limits were very fixed – you always had six or seven hour sessions and rapid games were always twenty-five or thirty minutes. Once the Fischer clock was introduced all kinds of tournaments had different time limits and different increments, it became totally random. I think that the time control is no longer a sacred thing; it's something that is varied at every event. It's just very bad. If they can get TV then that's fine, but if they can't then why change the time limit? It makes no sense. Almost all of the players are united on this, the vast majority. I really don't think that any players are interested in this new time control. I think that it's basically a bad move.

What do you think of the FIDE doping policies?
Well, I don't think drug testing is particularly important; there just aren't any substances that can be good for a chess game. You don't really know when you sit down how long the game is going to last, how the game is going to go, whether it's going to be tactical or whether there's going to be a long ending, so I don't really believe that there are any such beneficial substances. I think that the main reason FIDE is doing this is the wish to get chess into the Olympic Games. I'm not a big fan of this, either, I don't think that it's a priority at all. I don't think that they have any interest in drug testing other than to make chess eligible for the Olympic Games, but it is definitely a bad idea for the players.

How important in your success are determination and belief in yourself?
I think that all good players believe in themselves. If you have a period of bad results that will of course put a few doubts in your mind, but you've always got to have inner belief, even when things are going wrong. Then you'll always be able to play better. You'll believe that you're a good player, a decent player, even if you're losing a lot of games. You've just got to get on with it. Sometimes a tournament or individual events don't go well, but you've just got to bounce back at the next one.

You have the reputation of being ice-cool at the board. How do you avoid the nerves that others feel at crucial moments?

Everyone feels nervous, but that's just natural. I don't react too much at the board and I think that's why people think I'm very cool. Somehow I just don't normally react very much when I'm playing, I just look the same, or so I've been told. I don't really notice it, but lots of people have said that it's hard to judge how I'm doing by how I look. But on the other hand, I can't really say that when I see other players I can tell exactly what they're feeling by how they're looking. It's just a chess thing; I just sit there and look indifferent. It's just when I'm playing. I probably don't do it the rest of the time. I just get into a certain zone.

I've never seen you get into time trouble. Are you simply more methodical with your allocation of time per move?

It's not true that I'm never in time trouble; it happens to everyone sometimes, but I do take a practical view. I believe that, in some positions, if you've been thinking for a certain amount of time then you simply have to move, you can't sit there forever. I think you often tend to judge positions early on as being very critical, but a lot more can still happen in the game. If you spend all your time on this position, when you don't particularly like it, then later on, when you might get chances to save the game, you can tend to go wrong because you are short of time. You have to give yourself a chance and try and make moves if you can.

Do you still believe that chess is 'really all a question of openings'?

Well, the opening is a key part of the game, particularly now you have computer databases available, computer assistance. If you can control the opening, remain in your preparation, get the advantage there, very often that is an important factor. A lot of opening preparation now goes into the middlegame. I think that working on your openings is more relevant than working on any other stage of the game because the ending is an area that you may not reach if you don't work on your openings. That's the logical way to work on chess. Equally, there is a lot more to it. There are a lot of players who have very good openings but are unable to be as strong later on and, often, when people play them, they tend to catch them out by playing offbeat openings. Chess isn't purely openings, but it is a very important part of the game, especially now, as there is so much information available.

Do you ever lose sleep before crucial games? And what effect does this have on your play?

I sleep a lot more during tournaments than I do when I'm not playing. It's just a question of trying to save your energy for when you're playing, but I don't really lose sleep that often. I don't really worry about it; it's more if you have a bad game, that's the most difficult thing. If you have a really bad game there's no way to completely forget about this by the next day, but you've got to do it as best you can.

You have all of these amazing qualities as a chess player, but what do you consider to be your greatest strength?

Like I said before, I think that I'm a pretty practical player and I'm pretty reasonable in all aspects. I don't have too many obvious weaknesses. I think I'm sort of an all-round player and that's perhaps my greatest strength.

At the other end of the spectrum, what was your worst blunder and what did you learn from it?

I don't know if I've got one particular blunder, but I think that in general I've learnt from the mistakes that I've made over a period of time. Particularly in tactical positions, where my concentration levels weren't high enough. I know now the types of positions that I tend to make errors in, particularly calculation, heavy positions; I dedicate more time to these positions and decisions and check things more carefully. There's not one particular blunder, but a number of games and a pattern that I saw recurring.

But I suppose that one of my worst blunders was playing for England in the Olympiad in Novi Sad (1990), where I dropped a rook against Kozul. He played for the 'home' team so I was in front of about three or four thousand spectators, which was rather tough. Then I was benched for the rest of the competition. It was a little bit brutal but I was probably worse anyway, so it wasn't that bad.

(In Michael and his father Bill's book, Chess in the Fast Lane*, Bill recalls the consequence of this loss: 'Michael's disappointment sent him looking for revenge against Kozul. This can be a very dangerous approach, although on this occasion it worked well and Michael registered three wins against this opponent in the next twelve months, although he would gladly have swapped any of them with the Olympiad result.')*

How important are tournament conditions to your play?

Obviously that's got to be a factor. I'm not really bothered about playing conditions in the tournament hall, that really doesn't bother me, bad light, all this kind of thing. Maybe if it's really hot I don't like it too much, but somehow things like lighting never really bothered me. But the hotel is really important. If you're going to be staying somewhere for a couple of weeks, if you've got a bad hotel room, that's going to be a problem. If it's very noisy, or very hot, if in general there are problems with the hotel, that can be annoying. Normally the hotels that I stay in are pretty reasonable. You don't really need deluxe conditions, just something fairly normal, and usually the organisers do their best.

What is your most entertaining chess story?

I'll talk about the time when England won the gold medals in Pula in the European Team Championships 1997, which was a very special moment in my career, anyway. It all started off slightly disastrously, when we headed off to Heathrow airport and, unfortunately, the British Chess Federation (BCF) had booked us tickets on a flight that wasn't actually going, or at least not for two or three days, which would have been a bit tricky with the first round starting the next day. We were all rushing around. Dave Norwood was the captain and he went off to British Airways and tried to persuade them to give us free tickets. In the end we managed to find some seats on a Croatian airline and I put all the tickets on my visa card, as no one else had a high enough limit. The BCF did repay me; I have to say that, to be fair to them.

Although it started off pretty badly, it all went well from then and we were leading going into the last round and managed to win on tie-break against the Russians. There was also another thing that happened. At this time Tara was at home and she was basically filling in the pond in the garden. And on the day that we were actually winning the gold medal on tie-break she found the Koi carp that I now have over there, Alamo.

(Mickey points to his huge fish tank, and the massive Koi Alamo, which always has a calming and somewhat hypnotic effect on dinner guests).

So I think that it was finding the fish that enabled England to win the European Team Championship.

One of my most recent money-making ideas is chess Trivial Pursuit. Would this appeal to you or do you like to completely separate chess and personal time?
I'm not too big on thinking about chess when I'm not playing or working on it, but it does sound like it might be fun. I don't think that I'd play too often but I might try it a couple of times.

Do you seek to find beauty or simply victory?
I'm not interested in beauty too much when I'm playing; I'm just looking to win the game.

What do you consider to be your best game?
There aren't too many games that I consider to be great from start to finish; it's difficult to say. I quite like my game against Ivanchuk, quite a few years ago now, just because at some stage he ends up in zugzwang with quite a lot of pieces on the board. It's quite pretty. I would hope to play a better one, but wouldn't we all.

Michael annotated this game himself in *Chess in the Fast Lane*. I have included some of his original annotations, which are marked MA and written in italics.

1 e4 e5 2 ♘f3 ♘c6 3 ♗b5

The Ruy Lopez represents one of White's most logical replies to 1...e5. I think that every chess player who wants to improve should study the main lines of the Lopez. There is a delicious mix of tactics and strategy which would benefit everyone who played through the games of Karpov, Kasparov and Michael Adams himself.

3...a6

3...♘f6 has become more popular since Kramnik's successful adoption of it against Kasparov in their World Championship Match, but I doubt it will ever replace the old move played by Mickey in this game.

4 ♗a4 ♘f6 5 0-0 ♗e7 6 ♖e1 b5

These moves have been played by strong players for years and, at this stage, the two chess gladiators are simply going through the motions.

7 ♗b3 0-0 8 c3

The complexities of the Marshall attack can be avoided if White plays the slightly wimpy 8 a4, now known (somewhat obviously) as the 'anti-Marshall'. Although theoretically Black is doing fine in this line, psychologically it can be difficult for him to adjust as he doesn't get the easy attacking game so loved by advocates of the Marshall Gambit.

8...d5

Adams is one of the strongest Grandmasters to employ the Marshall on a regular basis. The patient manoeuvring associated with the closed Lopez is thrown out of the window as Black immediately seizes the initiative. The question is, will he get enough play for his sacrificed pawn? Theory is still undecided.

9 exd5 ♘xd5 10 ♘xe5

If White wants to try for any kind of advantage he must accept the proffered pawn. Otherwise Black will have freed his game at no cost.

10...♘xe5 11 ♖xe5 c6

The main line.

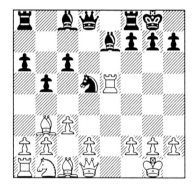

12 d4

12 d3 is a reasonable alternative, aiming to help control the potentially vulnerable light squares. Then 12...♗d6 13 ♖e1 ♕h4 14 g3 ♕h3 15 ♖e4 ♘f6 16 ♖h4 ♕f5 is a typical continuation, when White has stemmed the first wave of the attack but lags behind in development. Meanwhile, Black is ready to lash out on the kingside with ...g7-g5. Theory promises White a slight advantage but you need nerves of steel and a good knowledge of the position to play this line with either colour!

12...♗d6 13 ♖e1 ♕h4

Ivanchuk's kingside is without defenders so it is only logical for Adams to begin his attack.

14 g3

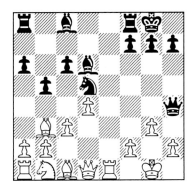

14...♕h3

Mickey can be quite satisfied with the first stage of the attack, having forced Ivanchuk into weakening the light squares in front of his king. This by itself is not enough to justify the pawn sacrifice, but he has many other cards up his sleeve, namely very active pieces and a large lead in development. Meanwhile, Ivanchuk can look forward to consolidating his material advantage once he gets his remaining pieces into the game.

15 ♗e3

This direct attempt to catch up on development is the most logical approach to the position. 15 ♖e4 is also possible, but here Black has no need to prepare 15...g5 as 16 ♗xg5 loses a piece to 16...♕f5.

15...♗g4 16 ♕d3

It is clearly vital for the white queen to stay in touch with the light squares on the kingside.

16...♖ae8

The common feature of most gam-

bits is the effortless way in which most of the pieces are involved in pursuing the initiative. The Marshall is no exception. The f8-rook is the only black piece currently without an active role but this can be remedied with a quick ...f5-f4.

17 ♘d2 ♕h5

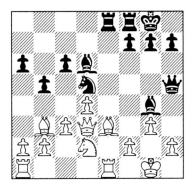

Cementing his grip on the h5-d1 diagonal. One idea is to play a timely ...♗e2, when White's queen may be embarrassed for squares. At the time this was a relatively new continuation. Theory had mostly concentrated on the more direct moves 17...♖e6 and 17...f5.

MA: I was trying to play the Spassky system (which would have been achieved by 17...♖e6 18 a4 ♕h5) but accidentally inverted the order of moves. I only realised this when I made my move because Vassily raised his eyebrows and sunk into thought. Strangely, after I played this move all the lights in the tournament hall went out! They were repaired fifteen minutes later, but Chukky continued thinking for about another 50 minutes before playing:

18 ♘f1

White fortifies the kingside defences, deciding that prevention is better than cure. The drawback is that the knight is very passively placed here and White has to abandon any pretence of battling for control of f3. 18 a4 is more robust, when 18...♗f5 19 ♕f1 ♗h3 20 ♗d1 ♕f5 21 ♕e2 c5 22 ♘f3 allowed White to keep an edge six years later in Morovic-Adams, Santiago 1997.

18...♖e6 19 ♗d1

The bishop returns to defensive duties, this time with the clear objective of exchanging off Black's light squared bishop.

MA: I do not like this move, after which Black should have very good compensation for his pawn. Normal is 19 a4.

19...f5

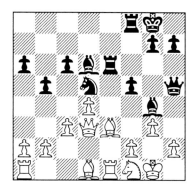

The natural follow up, as now there is little danger along the a2-g8 diagonal. The f-pawn can be used as a battering ram and, meanwhile, the f8-rook is called up for duty.

20 ♗xg4 ♕xg4 21 ♗d2 ♖g6

Adams is naturally eager to avoid any more exchanges and instead finds a menacing role for his rook on the king-side.

22 ♔g2?!

Ivanchuk dreams of reaching a favourable endgame with 23 ♕f3 but, as we shall see, there simply isn't time for this. 22 ♕e2 is relatively best, when the

game is finely balanced after 22...♕h3 23 f3 and White's queen is ready to evict her counterpart with ♕g2.

22...f4

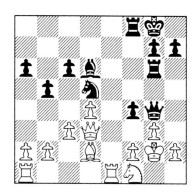

23 f3

Forced in order to prevent Black's pawn landing on f3, creating some very nasty threats. Note that 23 ♕f3?? ♕xf3+ 24 ♔xf3 fxg3+ wins for Black.

23...♕h5 24 g4 ♕h4

Timing is the key to every successful attack and here Mickey shows admirable restraint. Many players would be tempted to jump in with the immediate 24...♖xg4+? but the attack can be repulsed with accurate defence. I am sure that Ivanchuk was ready with the riposte 25 fxg4 ♕xg4+ 26 ♔h1 f3 27 ♘g3 ♗xg3 28 ♖g1!, turning the tables completely.

MA: I spent a lot of time looking at the tempting 24...♘f6 25 h3 ♕h4, but White has a good defence in 26 ♖e2 (26 ♖e6 is also possible but much less clear) 26...♗h6 27 ♔g1 when Black has no real way to proceed.

25 ♖e2

It turns out that he has no good defence to the threat of ...♖xg4, so Ivanchuk attempts to reinforce his second rank. After 25 ♔h1 ♖xg4 26 fxg4 f3

Black, who threatens ...♕f2, has an extremely strong attack.

25...♖xg4 + !

This tactical strike weakens White's king position and helps activate Black's remaining rook.

26 fxg4 f3 + 27 ♔h1

MA: I had totally failed to notice this, looking only at 27 ♕f3 ♖xf3 28 ♔xf3 ♕h3+ 29 ♘g3 ♘f6 or 29 ♔f2 ♗xh2, both with very good chances for Black. The text move is definitely better, although White's king will never be completely safe.

27...fxe2 28 ♕xe2 ♔h8

A very sensible move. White can do nothing about his kingside weaknesses so Mickey casually spends a couple of moves tidying up his own king position before launching the next wave of the attack. Prophylactic play now means that when Black's attack arrives White will have no meaningful counterplay.

29 ♔g1 h6 30 ♕g2 ♗f4

At first sight it looks a little odd to be offering to trade what is arguably quite a poor piece, but Mickey has seen that without White's dark-squared bishop the black knight will be even stronger.

31 ♗e1

Ivanchuk shows that he is perfectly

aware of the dangers involved in giving up the fight for the dark squares around his kingside. For example after 31 ♗xf4 ♘xf4 32 ♕xc6 ♕xg4+ 33 ♔h1 ♕e2 White's position is in danger of collapse.

31...♕g5 32 h3

MA: Both players were running a little short of time at this point and in particular the pace of Vasily's moves had increased. 32 h3 was flicked out as another solid quick move, but in fact the loss of time is rather critical. 32 ♖d1 had to be played.

32...♕g6

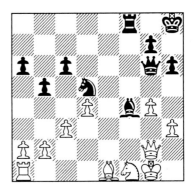

Mickey continues to probe his opponent's position without threatening anything dramatic. This approach often pays dividends, especially against an opponent under time pressure. This is because it is much easier to defend – and therefore react instantly – against direct threats.

MA: Once seen, a very obvious move, but it took me a while to stumble on it. None of the more obvious attempts at infiltrating on the dark squares really accomplishes anything but now that the queen controls the light squares the situation is very different. White's reply is forced to prevent ...♕d3.

33 ♖d1 ♗b8

It must have been agonising for Ivanchuk, playing against an opponent who simply won't reveal his hand. White knows he is going to be hit; he just doesn't know where or when!

34 ♖d2

White has little choice but to defend his second rank due to the threat of ...♘f4. Unfortunately, vacating the first rank gives Black a different avenue of attack. 34 ♗d2 is now well met by 34...♕c2, while 34 ♗g3 ♗xg3 35 ♕xg3 ♕c2 is also very unpleasant for White.

34...♕b1

Ouch! It is never pleasant to be probed along your own back rank.

35 ♗f2

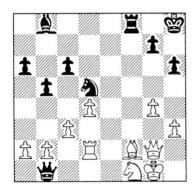

35...♔g8

Slow and painful torture! White is in virtual Zugzwang. All piece moves lose material, so White is simply handed back the move. Adams knows only too well that any reply serves to deteriorate Ivanchuk's position.

36 b3

The only (slim) chance is to try and generate queenside counterplay, as otherwise Mickey would simply wait for White to run out of pawn moves.

MA: The rest needs little comment as once the white rook leaves its defensive position, the roof falls in.

36...♗f4 37 ♖e2 ♘xc3

Black finally recoups his sacrificed pawn. With the positional gains he has made still in place, he now has a completely won game.

38 ♖e6

A final, desperate bid for counterplay.

38...♕xa2 39 ♖xc6 ♕xb3 40 ♖xa6 ♘e2+ 41 ♔h1 ♗b8

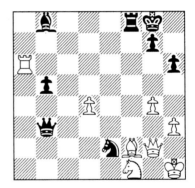

There are simply too many threats for White to contend with. He cannot defend his back rank, the threat of ...♘f4 and the black rook's pressure on the open file simultaneously. Something has to give.

42 ♗e1

There is little better, resignation being an option. 42 ♖b6 loses simply to 42...♘f4 43 ♕g3 ♕d5+ 44 ♔h2 ♗c7, when the threat of ...♘e6 is decisive.

42...♕d1 0-1

A fantastic display of sustained pressure by Michael Adams. To beat a super strong opponent with such a relentless display of controlled attacking was a splendid achievement. Ivanchuk must have been absolutely shell-shocked by the end.

What do you think is the best game ever played?

The following game played a decisive role in determining the winner of the PCA World Championships in 1995. Kasparov looked to be in trouble. He had thus far made absolutely no headway against Anand's Black defences and, after eight draws, had just fallen behind in the match in Game 9. Many players would have been demoralised by such a turn of events, but not Kasparov! He rolled up his sleeves and came out fighting! The result was a fantastic display of immaculate opening preparation.

Kasparov-Anand
PCA World Ch., New York 1995
Ruy Lopez

---

1 e4 e5 2 ♘f3 ♘c6 3 ♗b5 a6 4 ♗a4 ♘f6 5 0-0 ♘xe4

Anand had been successful with the Open variation against the Ruy Lopez in Game 6 and decided to repeat that opening choice. In hindsight it is easy to criticise this but, at the time, Anand must have been feeling pretty confident that his preparation was as good as Kasparov's.

6 d4 b5 7 ♗b3 d5

Black has had to compromise his pawn structure in order to guard against a disaster on the e-file, but in return gets active piece play not normally seen in the Ruy Lopez. After 7...exd4 we see why Black must take care to ensure the e-file remains closed, since after 8 ♖e1 d5 9 ♘c3! he already has big problems thanks to his exposed king.

8 dxe5 ♗e6 9 ♘bd2

The most precise move, popularised by Karpov. The threat of ♘xe4 discourages Black from playing the active 9...♗c5, which would now lead to an unpleasant endgame.

9...♘c5

The only way to try and exploit Kas-parov's omission of c2-c3. Anand avoids the exchange of his active knight and plans to plough straight through the centre.

10 c3 d4 11 ♘g5!?

An unbelievable move the first time you see it. White moves his knight to a square where it can simply be taken. However, capturing the knight does not guarantee Black an easy life – far from it! In fact, this was not the first time this surprising move had been uncorked in a world championship match. Karpov, using the idea of his trainer Igor Zaitsev, played this against Korchnoi in their 1978 match.

11...dxc3

It is easy to frown on this move now, but Anand had held Kasparov comfortably in the sixth game of the match and was blissfully unaware of the improvement that Kasparov had prepared for this game. 11...♗d5 is the latest try, when White's knight can continue on its journey with 12 ♘xf7!? ♔xf7 13 ♕f3+ ♔e6, when White has a strong attack for the sacrificed piece after both 14 ♕g4+ and 14 ♘e4. After 11...♕xg5 12 ♕f3 Black is more or less forced to return the piece with 12...0-0-0 as the greedy 12...♔d7 allows 13 ♗d5 ♗xd5 14 ♕xd5+ ♗d6 15 cxd4 ♘xd4 16 ♘c4.

12 ♘xe6 fxe6 13 bxc3 ♕d3

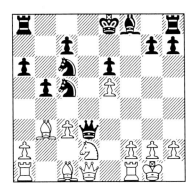

14 ♗c2!

Here Garry veers away, with great effect, from Game 6, where he tried the less ambitious 14 ♘f3. With ♗c2 White prepares a startling rook sacrifice that was originally devised by the tactical genius Mikhail Tal. Kasparov had prepared this blow in depth only the weekend before this game was played.

14...♕xc3 15 ♘b3 ♘xb3

Anand had a long think before playing this move and, indeed, it is hard to improve upon it. 15...♖d8 declines the rook sacrifice but after 16 ♗d2 ♖xd2 17 ♘xd2 ♘xe5 18 ♘b3 Black was worse in Khalifman-Hracek, Parnu 1996 in view of his weakened pawn structure.

16 ♗xb3

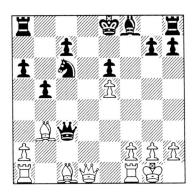

16...♘d4

Taking the rook immediately is tempting, but Anand must have feared both Kasparov's attack and his home preparation, as the champion was still 'blitzing' out his moves. 16...♕xa1 meets with 17 ♕h5+, giving Black an awkward choice between weakening his kingside and running with the king. After 17...♔d7 18 ♗xe6+ ♔xe6 19 ♕g4+ ♔d5 Black, as you might expect, loses rather quickly to 20 ♕d7+ ♗d6 21 ♕f7+ ♔xe5 22 ♕xg7+ etc. This leaves 19...♔f7 20 ♕f3+ ♔e6 21 ♕xc6+, when Black is really made to pay for leaving his king in the centre: 21...♗d6 22 exd6 ♕e5 and now 23 ♗b2! is the killer blow which ends Black's hopes of defending the king. Black can struggle on but he is doomed after 23...♕xb2 24 ♖e1+ ♔f6 25 ♕f3+ ♔g6 26 ♕g4+ ♔h6 27 ♖e6+. Now Black can only avoid a quick end by giving up his queen for nothing with 27...♕f6 (27...g6 allows mate in five with 28 ♕f4+ ♔h5 29 g4+ ♔h4 30 ♕h6+ ♔xg4 31 ♖e4+ etc.) 28 h4 g6 (the only way to prevent ♕g5 mate), but now 29 ♖xf6 is clearly hopeless for Black.

In the event of 17...g6 18 ♕f3 White utilises the pin on the h1–a8 diagonal. Then 18...♘d8 19 ♕f6 ♖g8 20 ♗xe6 wins for White as Black cannot deal with the threats of ♗d7+, (followed by e6+, winning the queen), ♗xg8 or, in the case of 20...♖g7 21 ♗a3, the double attack on Black's queen and bishop. Even worse is 18...0-0-0 due to 19 ♕xc6 ♕xe5 20 ♕xa6+ ♔b8 (20...♔d7 21 ♗b2!) 21 ♗e3, when White has a devastating attack.

17 ♕g4 ♕xa1

What else?

18 ♗xe6

The sight of Garry Kasparov confidently playing his moves more or less instantly (and sacrificing material in the process) must have been very intimidating for Anand who, by now, and very unusually, was falling far behind on the clock.

18...♖d8

18...♘xe6 loses immediately to 19 ♕xe6+ ♗e7 20 ♗g5. Complicated is 18...♕c3, but White gets the upper hand with 19 ♗d7+ ♔f7 20 ♗e3 ♗c5 21 e6+ (the key move as the e-pawn proves to be a monster) 21...♔g8 (21...♔f8 22 ♕f4+) 22 e7 g6 23 ♕e4 ♔g7 24 ♕e5+ ♔f7 25 ♗e6+ and Black must give up his queen to stem the attack.

19 ♗h6

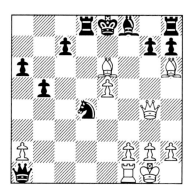

Very nice! White wants to deflect the g-pawn in order to mate after ♕h5+.

19...♕c3

Anand has to return material in order to try to hold back the tide. 19...♕xf1+ leads Black down a very dark alley: 20 ♔xf1 gxh6 21 ♕h5+ with mate next move.

20 ♗xg7 ♕d3

Providing much needed protection to the light squares on the kingside. Black has saved his king but has had to pay a heavy material price. 20...♗xg7 is again met by the devastating 21 ♕h5+.

21 ♗xh8 ♕g6

21...♘e2+ looks tempting, but grabbing more material should be the last thing on Black's mind. After 22 ♔h1 ♘g3+ 23 hxg3 ♕xf1+ Black wins an exchange but his queen is a very long way from home: 24 ♔h2 ♕d3 25 ♗f5! (cutting the queen off from her king) 25...♕c4 (25...♕d1 26 f3) 26 ♕h3 and White has a decisive lead, with Black's king unable to survive in the long-term.

22 ♗f6 ♗e7 23 ♗xe7 ♕xg4

Trading queens is absolutely essential if Black is to have any hope of survival. 23...♔xe7 24 ♕h4+ ♔e8 25 ♗g4 leaves Black suffering.

24 ♗xg4 ♔xe7

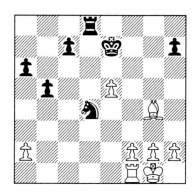

25 ♖c1

Kasparov finally started thinking here, using the valuable time that he had gained with his opening novelty. Prophylaxis is first on the agenda. It is vital to hinder Black's queenside counterplay based on ...c5-c4. While Black is busy defending his backward c-pawn White is given time to advance his kingside pawn majority.

25...c6 26 f4 a5 27 ♔f2

Centralising the king is a key requirement of good endgame play. And, indeed, the monarch rushes forward to support the advanced pawns.

27...a4 28 ♔e3 b4

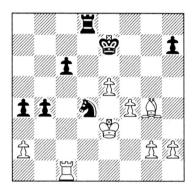

29 ♗d1

Kasparov plays the final phase of the game superbly, skilfully restraining Anand's counterplay. 29 ♖c4 looks like the obvious move but it allows the devilish trap 29...a3, when 30 ♖xd4 ♖xd4 31 ♔xd4 b3 actually wins for Black!

29...a3

The only chance. 29...b3 30 axb3 axb3 31 ♖b1 sees White pick up the b-pawn.

30 g4

With Black's pawn avalanche on the queenside contained Kasparov is free to go back on the offensive.

30...♖d5 31 ♖c4

The queenside pawns are overextended and impossible to defend.

31...c5 32 ♔e4

The king proves his worth in the centre of the board, forcing the enemy rook into an abject retreat, when White can win the c-pawn.

32...♖d8 33 ♖xc5 ♘e6

33...b3 is also hopeless: 34 ♗xb3 ♘xb3 35 axb3 ♖a8 36 ♖c7+ ♔f8 37 ♖c1 a2 38 ♖a1, followed by advancing the kingside pawns, should win trivially for White.

34 ♖d5

Black cannot contemplate exchanging rooks.

34...♖c8

34...♖xd5 35 ♔xd5 ♘xf4+ 36 ♔c4 and White rounds up the remaining queenside pawns, leaving Black with a hopeless task.

35 f5 ♖c4+ 36 ♔e3 ♘c5 37 g5

There is no way of stopping White's pawns.

37...♖c1 38 ♖d6 1-0

A wonderful display of the power of opening preparation, which few of us could ever hope to emulate. Anand was simply lost before Kasparov finished remembering his homework! All that remained was for Garry to show that he could also play the endgame flawlessly, and Anand was left stunned. After this game Anand never properly recovered from the destruction of his main defence to 1 e4.

What would be your pearl of chess wisdom?

Be objective about your strengths and weaknesses!

CHAPTER TWO

Yasser Seirawan

For many people Yasser needs no introduction. He is well known on the American domestic and international chess circuits as both an excellent player and lecturer. Anyone who has ever attended one of his lectures and listened to his commentary will know that his enthusiasm and humour bring games to life in a way that no one else can even come close to.

In 1978, he became U.S. Junior Champion, going one better the following year to win the World Junior title, which he has described as the biggest 'buzz' ever. 1980 saw him achieve his Grandmaster title, closely followed by an historic win over Karpov, the first tournament victory for an American over a reigning world champion since Alekhine succumbed to Dake in 1932.

In 1983 Yasser brought previously unknown glamour to the chess world when he appeared in *Cosmopolitan* magazine as their September Bachelor of the Month. This publicity led to him receiving literally hundreds of letters from smitten women – including Miss Hawaii – all of which he ignored. (I wouldn't say 'ignored' – many sent photos...YS)

In 1987, he founded International Chess Enterprises, which for many years published the award winning *Inside Chess* magazine. He is also the author of many successful books on strategy, tactics and the history of chess, and has recently saved the seemingly doomed U.S. Championships from cancellation, attracting new sponsorship from the likes of Boeing and Microsoft.

Yasser's powerful desire to win has led to him being the highest rated American player and a four-times U.S. Champion. He has represented the U.S. no less than nine times at Olympiads and has on several occasions been a World Championship candidate. However, his chess and life ambitions remain simple: he wants to play the best chess players in the world and be a well-educated, happy and contented person.

Another side to this energetic and committed chess player is his long running and very public dispute with FIDE and it's President, Kirsan Iljumzhinov. It has been a well-documented encounter and, as such, I felt that asking further questions about FIDE in my interview would not benefit this book. However, for those who have missed – or, perhaps, just want to revisit – the issues, below is an extract from an open letter which Yasser wrote to Kirsan Iljumzhinov:

'The purpose of the present open letter is to register my despair and disgust over the current plight of FIDE to highlight the urgent need for wholesale changes and a fresh start.

No international organisation can ever hope to satisfy all of the people all of the time, but the key problem today is infinitely more serious: FIDE is no longer satisfying any of the people any of the time. When did FIDE last take an imaginative, workable initiative that received even a modicum of support from the chess world? When did it last deal with a major issue or event without shooting itself in the foot? Why has it stood by impotently as support and respect for it has evaporated, even amongst its traditional supporters? When did it show any respect for the prestige of a game which is many centuries old? Above all, why has it allowed itself to become a laughing-stock through its serial incompetence?

Never has FIDE been in such chaos. Never has its reputation sunk so low. Never has it been so isolated from reality. Never, in short, has there been a greater or more urgent need for a fresh start. After all these years of mistakes piling upon one another, it is time to say enough is enough. The time has come when the interests of chess players can be furthered only if the full present FIDE leadership – and you first and foremost as President – resign your posts. I urge you to do so with immediate effect. It will then be the mammoth task of your democratically elected successors to begin work on re-establishing FIDE as a respectable, organised, one which helps rather than hinders the development of chess and seeks to restore the game's dignity world-wide.

On a closing personal note, I stress that I have no axe to grind about the past, or any political ambition for the future. My sole interest remains what is in the interests of chess players of all levels throughout the world. The record shows that although I have never hesitated to criticise FIDE when necessary, I have sometimes found myself almost alone among masters and writers in defending it. Mr. President, it is time for you and your board to step aside.

On behalf of chess,

IGM Yasser Seirawan

(Written 12th June 2000)

Tell me about yourself and your early chess career?

Well, I was born March 24th 1960 in Damascus. At that time, Syria was in the midst of civil unrest, so my family purchased passports on the black market and escaped to Nottingham, England, before emigrating to Seattle in 1967. My mother is British and even now, she still has her British accent. You can take the girl out of the country, but you can't take the country out of the girl.

I didn't start to play chess until 1972. I was completely awful, but being so competitive my one desire was to beat my paraplegic neighbour David Chapman, who actually taught me the game. I mean, I would play 1 h4 d5 2 ♖h3 and he would, of course, capture my rook with 2...♗xh3. At which point I wouldn't recapture the bishop, oh no; I would bring my other rook out with 3 a4 e5 4 ♖a3. Then he would take that rook too. My rooks were never around for very long and because of this, it was only after about eighty games that I discovered castling.

I think that everybody goes through this initial unsuccessful period, but I was getting incredibly frustrated. I think that throughout the summer I lost three hundred consecutive games to David. He just beat me like a drum. In the end I asked him where he learned chess and he told me about a coffee shop where people went to play. So, I went there, hoping for some success, but these people also beat me. I mean if David beat me badly, these people totally destroyed me. I had no chance. So, I continued to lose game after game after game.

One day I came home and played David and I got a draw, which was an enormous victory. In hindsight I would say that David was about a 1200 Elo player. These days we tend to disparage anyone below 2700 Elo, but to my mind someone like David was a really good player. At 1200, players know a lot of different openings, they know to control the centre, how to develop their pieces, back rank checkmates etc. and this is really sophisticated stuff. So, I got my draw and I thought that this was really wonderful.

Around about this time I became aware of the existence of the Washington Chess Federation. I also realised that there was a chess magazine and that, most importantly, you could write down the moves of the game. I played in my first tournament, where of course I lost four games out of five. But what was extremely important to me was that I won a trophy, the under sixteen trophy. Of course, I thought that I was most deserving. It was years before I realised that I was the only under sixteen in the event. *(Yasser has the endearing quality of always laughing heartily at his own jokes and chuckles to himself for a moment)*

To this day I can clearly remember my parents turning on the Johnny Carson show one night to hear them announce their special guest, 'The American who has just won the World Chess Championships, Bobby Fischer.' How can he be the World Champion, I thought, he hasn't beaten me! Everybody in my neighbourhood could beat me, but Bobby hadn't. So, I continued to play. I played badly but I still continued. I played more and more chess and got more enthusiastic. At 1300 USCF (United States Chess Federation grade) I was extremely overrated, having only won one game. But by 1975, with sheer perseverance, I was really pushing expert level, 2000 USCF.

My biggest hurdle was 2200, to become a Master. My rating went up and down but I just couldn't break through the barrier. Late 1975 I played in my first Grandmaster tournament and had a phenomenal tournament performance rating of 2500.

So, I finally reached 2300 and I thought, wow, now I'm really overrated, but I never fell below 2300 again.

In 1978 I won the U.S. Junior Championship and also played in my first World Junior Under-21 event. I was so happy to be sitting next to my little American flag and be playing the 'evil Soviet empire.' I played the Soviet hero Artur Yusupov and he killed me. I felt that I had let my country down and I vowed next year I would do better, which I did. I won the gold medal! This was in general a very important achievement, not because of the personal power it gave me in terms of self-confidence, but it meant that I received invitations to play in tournaments that otherwise, as a 2600 Grandmaster, I would not have been invited to.

My career moved on and as a 19-year-old I had some excellent results, which meant that I received my Grandmaster title. I do feel that I had an advantage over many other players because of my personality. I draw people towards me, opponents who I've beaten and those who've beaten me. I was very fortunate in a sense because I had a group of people who circled around me and would say things like: 'Yas, will you come and look at something? Now, this is a basic Philidor's position, don't you know how this works? Please make sure that you get this one down, will you.' This was another important stage in my development that started as a twelve year old and really continued until I was working with Victor *(Korchnoi)*. It was as if I had a series of teachers and I think that this learning and study was extremely good for me.

In 1980 I started working with Victor Korchnoi, who actually paid me to be his second. It was a remarkable time and I really want to thank Victor deeply for the tutelage and training that we had, for basically an eighteen month period. After this training I started to play in major world internationals, world cups, candidate matches, things like that. I really had become a world-class player.

How would you describe your own style of play?

I consider myself to be a positional player, but that's too one-sided. I think that I'm a strategical player. I always have a grand strategy and I'm pretty good with tactics in terms of the watchdogs of strategy. I truly admire Karpov as a chess player. I think that his games are an extraordinary example of strategical mastery and yet I can't play like him and I don't think that anybody else can either. Then you look at the games of Garry Kasparov and he has both strategical and tactical play that is inimitable. I can understand the games, but I can't even come close to playing like that and I consider myself to be a very strong Grandmaster.

I'm also a materialist and proud of it. I'm a material boy, living in a material world. The best thing about playing is taking your opponent's pieces. You've gotta like that, that's a fun part of the game. I was playing this five year old, she was so sweet, she took my queen and the smile on her face would have melted anyone's heart, it was just gorgeous. When I gave her checkmate and the tears started pouring I was devastated, I'd checkmated this poor little girl. But when she remembered that she'd taken my queen, the sun came out again. So definitely, one of the best bits is taking your opponent's pieces. Fundamentally, I live from a materialistic perspective.

If you wanted to, would it possible to deliberately alter your playing style?

You can without question change your style. I think that to a great extent your style is dictated by your choice of openings. For example, if you play the Dragon from a young age and you stay true to the Dragon, I'm sorry, but your style is going to be extremely sharp. You go from the Dragon to the Caro-Kann and your style will undergo a fundamental change.

Why did you decide to become a professional chess player?

I think that it's really a simple answer. I really, really enjoy the game so very much. It's full of endless possibilities, so endlessly entertaining. The other thing is that I really enjoy meeting other chess players and I believe that in the chess world I have some really enduring friendships. As a chess player I get to visit some wonderful places and meet some wonderful people, which is why I knew by the age of about sixteen that this was a cool game and something that I wanted to play professionally.

It's a great hobby, it's a great sport and I have a nice life. I enjoy the aspects of travel, mostly – well, there are always exceptions – and I'm lucky that I can do it professionally. Unfortunately, I feel that at this time chess professionals are going through some very testing periods *(financially)*. As attractive as the lifestyle may be, it's a risky one. It really is rather sad when you think that this is a sport, a game that really strengthens the mind and forces responsibility and reasoned thought. It's one of the few things that does that.

Chess is an intelligent game, simply not marketable to the general population. It's too much like hard work and people are simply not prepared to work for their leisure. Here in America one of the reasons that the big sports – football, baseball and basketball – are so popular, is because of people like Michael Jordan. He's not just a cool person; he makes $47 million a year. And here, that makes you a hero, whether or not you score the winning shot. If our success is based on financial means, society will unfortunately keep saying, loser, loser, to the chess players. It makes playing chess professionally very hard. Sometimes I feel like saying 'OK mum, I'll go back to school and become a doctor.'

'I would love to see chess elevated in the United States but quite frankly it is a very, very uphill struggle. Chess really could do a lot of good for boys and girls, for Americans, just to get them to use their minds. But we overlook that, instead we insist on breaking our bones in boxing and crippling ourselves in other sports. It's very sad. I would like to be a catalyst, a trigger person, or just a cog in the wheel to get that awareness moving.' Taken from an interview with Yasser on Kasparovchess.com

So, what needs to change?

In the U.S. there are about 90,000 United States Chess Federation (USCF) members. These players have collectively bought about 1,000 of my books. However, as an author I have sold over 300,000 books, in America alone. So, I sit down and say, the USCF members aren't buying my books, who is? I think that the USCF is really missing the boat in terms of people who play chess. I feel that the chess world is not friendly or embracing enough to attract and retain the vast majority of people who play chess. The vast majority of players in America do not join the USCF. They continue to play in the parks and the community centres, because they don't perceive that there are benefits to playing with others. Or they see the chess world as being too isolated or myopic. It's true, because if you go to a lot of chess clubs in the United States, you can still see the stale walls, the stale atmosphere, almost closed to fresh blood, because this is their space, their place and you are invading it.

It must have been dreadful for you as a girl playing chess. Not only are you butting heads against this type of atmosphere, but also you receive sexual remarks. This really does upset me, because I think of chess as a sport that should allow women and men to compete equally. You shouldn't have to face any extra worries or fears as a woman. You should be able to walk into a chess tournament and not only feel a sense of empathy but a sense of friendliness. Let's celebrate; a woman wants to join our club. Oh no, there's no celebration to discuss here; we're going to pound her into submission until she leaves us alone.

Obviously in Georgia, I mean how wonderful is that – women are not merely encouraged, they have so many heroines to inspire them. There are so many great Georgian women. It is such a sad testament to the world of chess that women are more than half of society and yet are actively discouraged from playing chess. Well, I'm sorry boys, but we're screwing it up, we're doing it wrong. There needs to be a slap in the face and a cold day of reckoning:

a) We're not marketing ourselves right.

b) Our image sucks.

c) We have to reposition ourselves wholly from the ground up. If we ever want to reach 'd', which is a level of success.

But surely, it's difficult to change both the chess players themselves and the external view that others have of chess players.

I think that the answers are actually very simple. Society is changing, take this little girl here *(points to a tiny six-year-old girl who, with an expression of intense concentration, is analysing at a board that's almost as big as she is)*, she's doing something that in many countries she just wouldn't be allowed to do. Sexual discrimination would have prevented her from learning chess at all. She'd have been told that success constitutes finding a nice boy to take care of her. Today I think things are different. We are teaching our girls that they are legitimate human beings and they can do what they want. I mean, listen, it sounds stupid. It's not all men are created equal, it's all men and women are created equal. I consider Judit Polgar to be a godsend. She is a personable, beautiful, charming lady who speaks five or six languages. We should feel so blessed to have this person in our lives. So let's do our utmost to see that she and other ladies are attracted to chess.

I also think that the image of chess can be changed with the success of players such as Vishy *(Anand)* and Mickey Adams. Vishy is a hero to millions of Indians and I think you need to see that more and more. And twenty to thirty years ago Britain had Michael Stean, Tony Miles and John Nunn. These guys were scraping and clawing for a living. Now Mickey has come along and he's the first Brit to have earned £1 million from chess. And people think, how do you do it, how can I do it? I think that the more millionaires chess produces the better.

Now we've explored how to improve the chess world itself, how can we improve as chess players ourselves? What do you consider to be the best route to general chess improvement?

I really feel that the more you play, the better you get. I think that everyone has to realise – and Karpov wrote about it very well in *Karpov on Karpov* – that you have to lose about ten thousand games *(Yasser might have said a thousand; I'm not entirely sure)* before you can become a good player. I know now that I became a good player when I started losing well. In other words, the games weren't a wipe-out. I was showing resistance and both my opponent and I had actually played a good game. My opponents hadn't blundered and allowed me back into the game; they had fought for an advantage, ground me down and won.

Soon I started to lose brilliant games. Don't get me wrong, they were still painful losses, but this was when I started realising – hey, actually I'm not that bad. These people are really playing great chess and soon I'm going to be beating them!

And more specifically, my friend John is stuck at 2200 Elo, and desperately wants to better his play. What would your recommendations be?

Unfortunately his predicament is – well maybe the internet is changing this a great deal – but I feel that maybe he's not getting beaten badly enough. He needs somebody to really pound him into the turf. It's not much fun, but you know if you keep getting pounded by a 2500-2600 player and he's really taking you to the cleaners, your 2250 rating may not look so good, but before too long, you're going to get to 2350.

The point is, that you really need to be allowed to play those stronger than yourself so you can pick up ideas and see what their motivations are at the chessboard. I was around a lot of experts who literally drew me to them, but I wasn't around enough Masters who could draw me to their level. So, it wasn't until I was seventeen, until I became the World Junior Champion, that I could draw upon the masters. Again, I would say expand your circle to meet much stronger players.

How much time do you devote to chess study and how should you most effectively divide your study time?

First of all I'm a very poor example and I urge people not to imitate me under any circumstances. All the great sports stars say that come sleet or snow, whatever the weather, for example, you have to run two miles a day. They don't care if you're injured or you've got kidney failure, you still have to run. So they tough it out, they study and then they study some more.

I approach my study differently. First of all I don't like to work when I'm tired. I feel that I'll be wasting my time and I won't be true to myself. I want to come to my study period in the same way that you come from the shower, fresh. This way, I'm ready to burst out and absorb information. I also need to feel physically, emotionally and mentally in shape, so for the next five hours or so, I can have a good study session. My sessions are usually fairly long, as I don't absorb enough in short periods. I also like to arrange my day so that I won't be disturbed. It's very difficult to train and arrange your thoughts if the phone rings or if you have to go here and there. So, I would say that personally I take a structured approach and I come to the table mentally ready to absorb.

I also don't sit down and say, well, I really have this terrible weakness in rook and pawn endgames and I'm going to thrash my way through a massive chess endgame book. To me, this is a massive turn-off. I remember working with Grandmaster James Tarjan (Toejam to his friends – YS) in preparation for an Interzonal. It was 1979 and we were living in Hollywood. We would get up in the morning, jump in his VW Beatle, drive down to Venice Beach, drink at least three cappuccinos and watch incredibly scantily clad girls zoom around on roller-skates. I mean, God – we were in Hollywood, life was good. We would kind of stagger home mid-afternoon, just as the sun was getting unbearable and then study chess for four to six hours.

We'd make dinner, we were great cooks too. My mother's British as I said and can't cook to save her life *(I took great offence here on behalf of British women everywhere)*, so the children had to learn. James and I would cook every day, food that would literally turn a Mexican red. I mean we'd have some really great spicy food. We'd also have some great extra long study sessions, as we couldn't sleep after the spicy food. We studied the Sicilian Najdorf like this straight through for two weeks and we knew it inside out. We were literally boarding the plane to go, when we discovered a major flaw in a crucial line and we were heartbroken. I thought that we had wasted our time, but James said: 'Yasser, all study is good. Even if your analysis is bad, you're still analysing and even if that line was bad, we still learned a hell of a lot about the Sicilian Najdorf.' That's my basic philosophy of study. I want to have the feeling that I'm enjoying it.

I think that it's nice to study with others. It's not just the spirit of mutual camaraderie and adventure; you push one another, especially when you find a compatible personality to work with. You tend to bounce things off each other very well. Virtually all my training sessions degenerate into blitz sessions, which I really enjoy.

But guess what, we have a lot of fun and we're looking forward to the next study session.

If I'm on my own I like to study whole games. Specifically, I enjoy studying games of champions and top players. What I don't do now is just look at a particular opening. Let's say that I'm studying one of Kasparov's games, he's playing some incredibly sharp variation of the Sicilian and his opponent plays a move that I question because it feels wrong. It's at that point that I'll delve into my database and get a feeling for something else.

What is even better is to study games that players have annotated themselves. Not because I want to have all the answers, or have everything laid out on a plate for me, but because I want to know what and how they think. What I do is take an incredibly negative approach to their annotation. Specifically, I think: 'You're wrong. I don't care who you are, you're wrong, that annotation doesn't make any sense at all!' Then I try to prove that I'm right and they're wrong. Again, supporting the theory that any analysis is good.

I would also recommend using combination books. Personally, I don't set up the positions, but I literally feel them, I blindfold myself by closing my eyes and then I just solve the puzzle. I think that this is an extremely important skill to sharpen, so that when you come to your game, you will start to recognise patterns. I admit that there's also a bad aspect to this, because it's artificial. Because unfortunately no one taps you on the shoulder and says:

'OK White to move and win, or it's mate in five. Okay, here it is, it's a clearance sacrifice.'

So, that's a drawback. But in any case, I like to use these books

So, my study patterns are extremely poor. I don't sit down and pour over openings, then middlegames and endgames, because I don't want to put myself off. That's very important. If it becomes boring, then I know that I'm less desirous of the next session. For example if you invite me to dinner, and it's a horrible dinner the next invite that I receive, I'm less likely to turn up. And that's the way in which I like to approach my study. But if I'm really looking forward to it, then I'll book you. You know, I'll write you on my calendar.

How can you improve your analytical skills?
Your skills are like individual muscles and you have to work the right ones. I find that with calculation comes the need to do blindfold work. In other words, if you start to think about analysis and calculation, you can't move the pieces. You are absolutely prohibited from moving the pieces. So what I would say to you is that we're not going to analyse, we're not going to play blindfold, I'm going to read out moves to you and I want you to tell me how far you can hold the position until it becomes unclear. And the point is that if you're able to mentally picture the clarity of the game, even if it gets complicated with sacrifices, then you're going to improve.

So, I believe that being able to play blindfold chess is a very important skill, even though there are some criticisms of this. For example, in Wijk aan Zee, Ivanchuk had Kramnik cold, dead busted to the wall, got into time trouble, lost the game and was very emotionally hurt by his loss. He asked me to catch up with him at the hotel. The snow was falling and it was rather cold that night. There were these three figures, Garry *(Kasparov)*, his second and Vassily Ivanchuk. They were walking very slowly, so it was easy for me to catch up with them. They're talking in Russian; they're doing their Russian thing *(mimes the expressive hand gestures that we have come to associate with many Russian players)*. So Garry's listening to Ivanchuk's ideas, they don't have any chess set, they're just analysing blindfold. This goes on and on until they reach the hotel, by which time Ivanchuk is truly healed. It's like a miraculous surgeon has come along and taken away his pain. Then they all said goodnight. It was very endearing, a very sweet moment, but at the heart of it was the fact that they were playing blindfolded. They were moving the pieces mentally and calculating further and further after each move. So the more you improve your calculation, the less you have to rely upon the pieces.

How do you and other Grandmasters retain extremely high levels of concentration for such long periods?

I was once analysing with John Nunn a horrendous Benoni game that we'd played. He had offered me a draw in a better position *(for him)* and I hadn't realised, because I'd had my hands to my ears, trying to focus. After he'd offered me the draw I played on and won, so he was miffed that I'd refused his draw. Afterwards he said:

'So why didn't you accept my draw offer?'

'What?!' I replied, 'You offered me a draw, are you nuts?'

'You didn't hear me?'

'No, at that point I was thinking about something, but I got distracted. I can't remember the exact distraction, maybe the coffee sucked, there was a pretty girl, there was great food, whatever, but I got distracted.'

John, at this point, was looking extremely confused. I attempted to clarify for him.

'I was calculating, but then my calculation stopped because of this interference. So what, it happens to everybody.'

'Yasser,' he exclaimed, throwing his hands into the air, 'What are you talking about?'

'Look,' I continued patiently, 'I calculated this variation, something happened and I lost my concentration. Then I couldn't calculate any further because of this thing that had happened. Doesn't this ever affect you?'

At which point I started to understand his confusion, as he focused his gaze on me:

'No, I never lose my concentration. I just think straight through.'

My startled reaction – 'John, you're a robot. You must be the only person in the world who can concentrate straight through' – was maybe not the most polite, but it was extraordinary. I think it's amazing that anyone can have the ability to utterly concentrate and can say right, there it is, there's the solution, without their thoughts colliding.

I lose my concentration all the time. If others were honest, I think it happens to them too. I also have times of peaceful tranquillity, when I'm in a Zen-like state, I'm totally into the game and my concentration is unhindered. I hate it when I lose concentration. I would love to say that all you need to do is follow this pattern and then you can control your mind forever, but my mind is like a giddy colt. It's just fresh and spanky and goes frolicking about here, there and everywhere. I love it when this colt runs along the path that I want it to and I hate it when it jumps over ditches without my say so. But sadly, I'm not able to harness my concentration. I very often lose it during a chess game, but there are other times when I knuckle down and it works. Sorry, but I have no answer to the concentration question.

What chess books would you urge me to read?

My personal favourite, which I've had for years, is *Alekhine's Best Games*, a two volume series. What I can do is give you authors that I enjoy, as opposed to opening studies or something like that. I ate like cotton candy the books of Peres and Tal. I really like the writing style of Tal, but his mode of play used to drive me insane. There he is sacrificing the house and I'm trying to protect one square. Giving away a queen, are you nuts? I just don't know how to play like that. A famous story goes that school children in the Soviet Union were extremely relieved when Tal lost the World Championship return match to Botvinnik, as they could go back to protecting their pieces instead of sacrificing them. *(However, Tal himself said: 'There are two types of sacrifices: correct ones and mine')*

I admired the way that Tal played, but God, I didn't want to imitate him, or Alekhine or Peres. I just loved their style of writing and their explanation of why they chose a certain path. So, my chess heroes were always people of the day, Bobby Fisher, Ljubojevic, Anderson, Victor *(Korchnoi)*.

Explain the psychology of the draw offer?

I remember Grandmaster Andrew Soltis wrote an article called The Weapon of the Draw Offer, in *Chess Life*. You must get hold of this because it's a brilliant exposition. *(I tried, but couldn't locate it)* Draw offers can be crippling and I think that it's a very underestimated subject. The draw offer gives you an opportunity to think about all the scenarios within the game.

'I know that I'm better, but boy, a draw doesn't hurt me in the tournament, I could still win a prize and maybe even a trophy and even if I'm better I'm still a little behind on time. Unfortunately, now I've been thinking about it for so long, I'm way behind on time..'

So, the draw can really be a potent weapon. 'I can't accept a draw, I've got to win this game. I've got to prove that my position is better, so I've now got to sacrifice a piece.'

I would say that a draw offer can be a good idea but, unfortunately, what happens if it's taken, because then you lose the opportunity to win the game. Maybe you were better, but your opponent's more highly rated, you want to play for the win, but the demon on your shoulder says take the draw, so it can work both ways. Personally, I rarely offer draws, I usually only offer when I'm trying to secure a first position. Otherwise, I consider chess just a good opportunity to play.

What is your bedside book, chess or otherwise?
Definitely otherwise; I read novels before bed. At the moment it's John Grisham's *The Brethren*. I love all the legal intrigue. I also love science fiction. I don't like taking chess to bed.

I asked Yasser to tell me some jokes but, unfortunately, this is the only one that made it through the editing process. The others were extremely funny, but definitely unprintable.
In America, Doctors and Lawyers have a history of disliking each other. A Doctor gets on the plane, he's got his medical book and his stethoscope with him and he sits down in the window seat. Moments later two Lawyers, obviously reviewing case files, sit down next to the Doctor. After about an hour of flying, the Doctor says,

'Excuse me gentlemen, I'm going to get myself a drink of cola. Do you want anything?'

'Yes,' says the first lawyer, 'a drink of cola would be nice.'

'I agree,' says the second lawyer, 'thank you.'

Just after the Doctor has left to get his drink, the first lawyer spits really grossly into his shoe. The other lawyer looks at him, nods and does exactly the same in the Doctor's other shoe. After a few minutes the Doctor returns with the drinks and the flight continues. Just as the plane's coming in to land, the doctor puts his shoes back on. He immediately knows just what's happened, I mean yuck. So, shaking his head, he turns sadly to the Lawyers and says:

'Why is there always this conflict between us, between doctors and lawyers. You're trying to help the world, I'm trying to help the world, when are we going to start getting along. When are we going to stop spitting in each others' shoes and pissing into each others' coca-colas.

(At which point, Yasser laughs outrageously at his own joke for about a minute)

What do you consider to be your greatest chess achievements?
Becoming a Grandmaster was an extremely good achievement for me because it was something that I'd basically aspired to do from the moment I became a chess player. The other achievements that I suppose I'm most proud of are, just in the order that they come to mind, that I'm a nine times Olympic player, I've defeated both Garry Kasparov and Anatoly Karpov while they were reigning World Cham-

pions, if I were to add up all my scores against Challengers and World Champions, I'm at about 50%, I've been a World Junior Champion, I've been the U.S. Champion four times and I was also very proud of becoming a World Championship Candidate.

On another level I would say that I've kept chess enjoyable for others. If you've witnessed my lectures *(which I did and they're wonderfully entertaining)* you can see that I share my great enthusiasm for the game with other people.

What do you consider to be your best game?

Probably my game with Timman in *Winning Chess Brilliancies*. I really enjoyed it. It was just a really sweet game, brilliant flowing combinations, everything worked fantastically and I won the match.

I also really liked the game that I played in Sweden against Karpov. I have immeasurable respect for him. I defeated him in a way that was absolutely unique. He was Black and my first moves were c4, d4, e4, f4. I then proceeded to develop all my pieces, at which point he still had his rooks and knights on their original squares, nothing had moved. You just don't do this to Karpov. Those are the games that jump immediately to mind.

I also defeated Kasparov in a way that really enticed the audience to stand up and cheer, which was very nice. I've played in front of audiences all around the world and I've played some really nice games, but I've lost some really beautiful games too. In general, I just have a lot of pleasant memories.

Seirawan-Timman
Hilversum Match 1990
Nimzo-Indian Defence

---

1 d4 ♘f6 2 c4 e6 3 ♘f3 b6 4 ♘c3 ♗b4 5 ♕b3

This is Seirawan's pet system. The queen sortie prevents the typical Nimzo-Indian concept of Black doubling White's c-pawns, whilst at the same time attacking the bishop. The main drawback is that the queen is developed rather early.

5...c5 6 a3

White puts the question to the bishop since retreating will rule out the possibility of ...♘c6-a5.

6...♗a5 7 ♗g5 ♘c6

Typical of Timman's uncompromising style, he chooses the most aggressive continuation, attacking the d-pawn. However, the knight is somewhat vulnerable on this square (as we shall see) so a safer course is 7...h6, or 7...♗b7.

8 0-0-0

One of White's main ideas in this system, preparing active play on the d-file and breaking the annoying pin on the knight.

8...♗xc3 9 d5!

The only way to play for the advantage. By offering a pawn sacrifice Yasser seizes the initiative. 9 ♕xc3 plays into Black's hands after 9...cxd4 10 ♘xd4 ♘e4! 11 ♗xd8 ♘xc3 12 bxc3 ♘xd8, when White's crippled queenside pawns will be a weakness in the endgame.

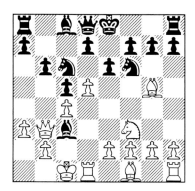

9...exd5?

According to the man himself this was over the board inspiration. Black opts for the riskiest and most complicated path, a decision he soon regrets. It is imperative to keep the f1–a6 diagonal closed, as will soon become apparent.

9...♘d4 won't do, either. 10 ♕xc3 ♘xf3 11 ♕xf3 is awkward for Black due to White's ability to build a big centre with e2-e4, while 10...♘e4 11 ♗xd8 ♘xc3 12 bxc3 ♘xf3 13 ♗c7 ♘g5 14 f3, threatening h2-h4, is better for White thanks to his strong centre and potential for occupying the central dark squares.

9...♗xb2+ grabs a hot pawn but White gets more than enough after 10 ♕xb2 ♘e7 (10...♘a5 11 e4 allows White an extremely dangerous pawn roller in the centre) 11 e4 with a dangerous initiative as 11...♘xe4 can be well met by both 12 d6 and 12 ♕xg7 ♖g8 13 ♕xg8+.

9...♗e5! is the move Timman had apparently prepared before the game. He should have stuck to his preparation as 10 dxc6 ♗c7 11 cxd7+ ♗xd7 12 g3 ♕e7 13 ♗g2 ♖d8 gives Black a fully equal game.

10 cxd5 ♗e5

The best choice at this juncture. 10...♗a5 simply misplaces the bishop and leaves him way out of the action. 10...♗d4, targeting the f2-pawn, is foolhardy because White can continue 11 dxc6 ♗xf2 12 cxd7+ ♗xd7 13 ♘e5, winning a piece.

11 dxc6 ♕e7

Stepping out of the pin on the d-file and defending the dark-squared bishop.

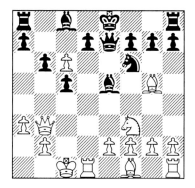

12 cxd7 +

In his book *Winning Chess Brilliancies* Yasser tells his readers that he was very tempted by 12 e4 but finally rejected it on account of 12...dxc6 13 ♘xe5 ♕xe5 14 f4 ♕c7, when he couldn't find a killer blow for White.

12...♗xd7 13 e3

This simple move, releasing the light-squared bishop, poses a real question to Black as to how he is going to complete development.

13...♖d8

13...0-0 14 ♘xe5 ♕xe5 15 ♗xf6 nets White a piece, 13...♗c6 14 ♗b5 ♖c8 15 ♗xc6+ ♖xc6 16 ♕a4 leads to a decisive material gain and 13...0-0-0 14 ♗a6+ ♔b8 15 ♘xe5 ♕xe5 16 ♗f4 wins the queen. 13...h6 allows the possible attractive finish 14 ♖xd7! ♔xd7 15 ♘xe5+

♕xe5 16 ♕xf7+ ♚c6 17 ♗f4! ♕f5 18 ♕c7+ ♚d5 19 ♕d6+ with mate next move. Finally 13...♗d6 14 ♗xf6 (14 ♗c4 ♗e6 15 ♕a4+ is also unpleasant for the second player, but perhaps after 15...♚f8 16 ♗xf6 gxf6 he has chances to hang on) 14...♕xf6 15 ♕d5 ♚e7 16 ♘g5 leaves Black with no good defence against the threat of ♘e4.

14 ♖xd7!

Paul Morphy made a similar sacrifice against the Duke of Brunswick in their famous game one hundred and thirty-two years earlier. Now a fellow American uses the same tactic.

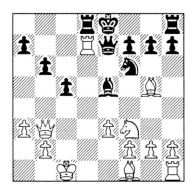

14...♖xd7

Absolutely forced. Black cannot afford to be greedy. 14...♚xd7 allows a king hunt of which Morphy himself would have been proud: 15 ♕a4+ ♚e6 (15...♚c8 allows White to win material while maintaining his attack with 16 ♗a6+ ♚b8 17 ♘xe5, as Black cannot recapture 17...♕xe5 due to 18 ♗f4) 16 ♗c4+ ♚f5 (the king can run but he cannot hide!) 17 ♕c2+ ♚g4 18 h3+ ♚h5 19 g4+ ♘xg4 20 hxg4+ ♚xg4 21 ♕e4+ ♗f4 22 ♕xf4.

15 ♗b5 ♗d6

Black rushes to block the d-file as he still cannot evacuate his king. 15...0-0? loses a piece to 16 ♗xd7 ♕xd7 17 ♘xe5.

16 ♖d1 0-0

Finally, but Black's problems are by no means over.

17 ♗xd7 ♕xd7 18 ♗f4

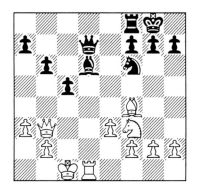

The pin on the d-file is deadly.

18...c4

Black tries a last trick. There is little choice, as knight moves lose instantly – 18...♘e8 runs into 19 ♕d5, while 18...♘e4 lasts slightly longer but White still gains material with 19 ♕d5 ♕a4 20 ♗xd6 ♖d8 21 ♘e5 ♘xd6 22 ♘c4, and the pin on the d-file is again decisive.

19 ♕c2

Controlling e4 and thus limiting Jan's options. 19 ♕xc4?? permits Black to turn the tables with 19...♖c8.

19...♘e8 20 ♘g5 f5

The only defence to both ♕h7 mate and ♘e4.

21 ♕xc4+

Now the pawn is safe to capture.

21...♚h8 22 ♗xd6 ♘xd6 23 ♕d5

The queen takes up a dominating post, again highlighting Black's plight on the d-file, whilst eyeing the vulnerable f7-square.

23...罝d8

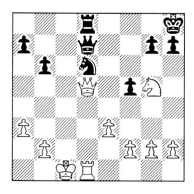

23...罝f6 fares no better in view of 24 豐a8+ 豐e8 25 豐xe8+ 公xe8 26 罝d8 罝f8 27 罝a8 with a completely winning endgame for White, and 23...罝c8+ 24 曾b1 罝c6 fails to 25 公f7+ (the black

queen is overloaded).

24 公e6!

Seirawan relates that he was almost tempted into 24 豐xd6? 豐c8+ 25 曾b1 罝xd6 26 罝xd6 – thinking that Black had no defence against 罝d8 followed by 公f7 – only to notice at the last moment that 26...曾g8 defends, 27 公e6 曾f7 putting Black firmly back in the game.

24...豐c8+ 25 曾b1 罝d7 26 豐xd6! 1-0

After Timman recaptures there is no way to prevent Yasser's rook arriving on d8, leaving him with an easy win. Seirawan is noted for his positional mastery, but in this game he showed that he is also a force to be feared in a tactical skirmish.

What do you consider to be the best game ever played?

Well, Kasparov-Topalov is an incredible game. It has immeasurable difficulty, brilliant creative play and a study-like finish. Massive complications, sacrifices, pin and counter pin – amazing. This game is everything a game of chess should be. And to my mind, the most important element of all is that the game is unclear for many moves. You just don't know who is winning! So many brilliant games are in many senses one-sided. This was a game that for a long time appeared to have no end. If you're looking for the best game of all time then it must be a candidate.

Kasparov-Topalov
Wijk aan Zee 1999
Pirc Defence

1 e4 d6

Topalov tries – some would say wisely – to avoid Kasparov's legendary opening preparation by trying the slightly offbeat Pirc Defence.

2 d4 公f6 3 公c3 g6 4 桅e3

Kasparov heads for an ambitious set-up that combines aggression with solidity.

4...桅g7

Fairly standard, but perhaps not the best move in the position. The point is that White is planning an attack based on 桅h6, which will weaken the dark squares around Black's kingside. Instead, by leaving the bishop at home with 4...c6!? Black can hope to save a tempo by being able to play ....桅xh6 in one move. For example after 5 豐d2 公bd7 6 桅d3 b5 7 公f3 e5 Black has reasonable chances of equalising.

5 豐d2 c6 6 f3

Kasparov opts for a slow build up,

hinting at a later kingside pawn storm. The most direct move is 6 ♗h6!?, but Kasparov might have feared home preparation.

6...b5

Naturally Topalov has been in no hurry to castle kingside. However, after this move there is no guarantee that his king will be safe on the queenside.

7 ♘ge2 ♘bd7 8 ♗h6 ♗xh6 9 ♕xh6 ♗b7

Topalov sensibly develops his pieces before challenging White in the centre. There is nothing wrong with the immediate 9...e5!?.

10 a3

A prophylactic move, taking the sting out of a possible ...b5-b4 before castling queenside.

10...e5

Black can really go for it with 10...a5 but this leaves his king without a safe haven, while White retains the option of running to the kingside.

11 0-0-0 ♕e7

Preparing to evacuate the king from the centre.

12 ♔b1 a6

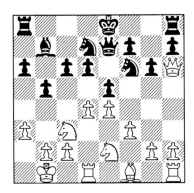

13 ♘c1

The only sensible way to unravel

without releasing the central tension. Kasparov anticipates that Topalov will castle queenside and notices that a5 is a potentially attractive square for his knight.

13...0-0-0 14 ♘b3 exd4

Topalov is not the sort of player to sit around meekly while his opponent goes about his plan. Instead he goes for immediate central counterplay.

15 ♖xd4 c5 16 ♖d1 ♘b6

The point of Black's idea, preparing the liberating ...d6-d5 pawn break.

17 g3

All good players try to utilise their redundant pieces and Kasparov is certainly not the exception to the rule, so he readies his bishop for entry into the game.

17...♔b8

Black decides to tuck his king away before commencing with central counterplay. 17...d5 leads to a slightly favourable position for White after 18 ♗h3+ ♔b8 19 exd5 ♘bxd5 20 ♘xd5 ♘xd5 21 ♘a5 when, although material is equal, Black's king safety will be a permanent cause for concern.

18 ♘a5

With 18 ♗h3 White might try to transpose to the variation in the previous note. However, true to his style, Kasparov tries to extract the utmost from every position. He can already envisage the rich combinational possibilities but, objectively, this very natural looking move is probably not the best.

18...♗a8 19 ♗h3 d5 20 ♕f4+ ♔a7 21 ♖he1

Kasparov is trying to lure Topalov into opening up the position, when the situation of Black's king will again become relevant.

21...d4

Practically forced as the alternative 21...dxe4 is exactly what Kasparov is looking for: 22 fxe4 (threatening ♘d5) 22...♘xe4?? 23 ♘xe4 ♖xd1+ 24 ♖xd1 ♗xe4 25 ♖e1 (threatening ♘c6+ as well as the bishop) 25...♖e8 26 ♖xe4! ♕xe4 27 ♕c7+ ♔a8 28 ♘c6 and Black can resign. Nor does 22...♖xd1+? 23 ♖xd1 ♘xe4 24 ♖d7+ ♘xd7 25 ♕c7+ help Black, so 22...♘h5 is relatively best, when White holds the advantage after 23 ♕f2.

22 ♘d5

The only way to make sense of his previous play.

22...♘bxd5

22...♘fxd5? leaves Black with no good way to defend his seventh rank after 23 exd5.

23 exd5 ♕d6

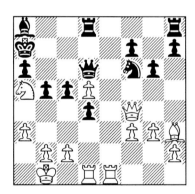

At first sight, it may appear that Kasparov has been too optimistic. The d5 pawn looks seriously weak and the endgame holds no pleasure for him. However, it is in such situations that Kasparov all too frequently demonstrates his true genius.

24 ♖xd4!!

An absolutely amazing monster of a move, which must have come as a total surprise to the Bulgarian super-grandmaster.

24...cxd4?

Topalov takes up the gauntlet and challenges Kasparov to prove his sacrifice. It turns out that Kasparov's concept is correct and Topalov should therefore have left the gauntlet where it was. The 'boring' 24...♔b6! is a better option, when it is doubtful that Kasparov has any better than the retreat 25 ♘b3.

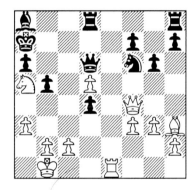

25 ♖e7+!!

The sacrifice of the second rook is obligatory, but it is spectacular nonetheless. 25 ♕xd4+? ruins all of White's good work because Black can defend with 25...♕b6! 26 ♖e7+ ♘d7 27 ♖xd7+ ♖xd7 28 ♕xh8 ♖xd5 with a decisive material lead.

25...♔b6

The second rook cannot be accepted as 25...♕xe7? 26 ♕xd4+ ♔b8 27 ♕b6+ ♗b7 28 ♘c6+ mates. Alternatively 25...♔b8 is dismantled by a series of accurate blows: 26 ♕xd4 ♘d7 27 ♗xd7 ♗xd5 28 c4 ♕xe7 29 ♕b6+ ♔a8 30 ♕xa6+ ♔b8 31 ♕b6+ ♔a8 32 ♗c6+

♗xc6 33 ♘xc6 and Black cannot both prevent mate and save his queen.

26 ♕xd4+ ♔xa5

The queen cannot yet help the king since 26...♕c5 is well met by 27 ♕xf6+ ♕d6 28 ♗e6! ♗xd5 29 b4 with a decisive attack.

27 b4+ ♔a4

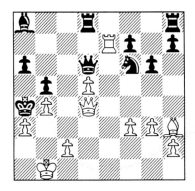

28 ♕c3

There may be another win with ♖a7 but Kasparov's move proves equally effective.

28...♕xd5

The only defence as 28...♗xd5? 29 ♔b2 leaves Black powerless against ♕b3+.

29 ♖a7 ♗b7

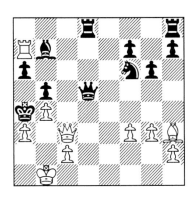

29...♖d6 overloads the rook and in-

vites 30 ♔b2, when ...♕d4 is no longer possible.

30 ♖xb7 ♕c4

Black is clearly intent on trading queens but he will not get his wish. The alternative 30...♖he8 runs into 31 ♖b6 ♖a8 32 ♗f1, when Black is struggling to meet the threat of the deflecting ♖d6, for example 32...♘d7 33 ♖d6, and White wins.

31 ♕xf6

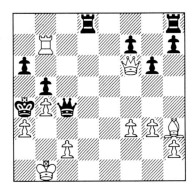

31...♔xa3

In the heat of the battle Topalov, understandably, misses his last chance. After 31...♖d1+ 32 ♔b2 ♖a8 33 ♕b6 ♕d4+ 34 ♕xd4 ♖xd4 35 ♖xf7 a5 36 ♗e6 axb4 37 ♗b3+ ♔a5 38 axb4+ ♔b6 (38...♖xb4 39 c3) 39 ♖xh7 White should be (technically) winning, although there is still a long way to go.

32 ♕xa6+ ♔xb4 33 c3+!

Forcing the king further into the jaws of the beast.

33...♔xc3 34 ♕a1+ ♔d2

Compulsory, unless Black wants to lose his queen immediately: 34...♔b4 35 ♕b2+ ♔a5 (35...♕b3 36 ♖xb5+) 36 ♕a3+ ♕a4 37 ♖a7+.

35 ♕b2+ ♔d1

35...♔e3? 36 ♖e7+, while 35...♔e1

36 ♖e7+ ♔d1 37 ♗f1! is the same as in the game.

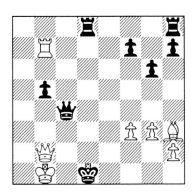

36 ♗f1!

White continues to find the only path to victory. Black's queen is deflected from the defence of c2.

36...♖d2

36...♕xf1 is clearly hopeless in view of the continuation 37 ♕c2+ ♔e1 38 ♖e7+ etc.

37 ♖d7!

And now the rook is deflected from its defensive duties, setting the stage for a fantastic finish to an absolutely phenomenal game.

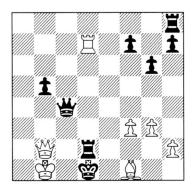

37...♖xd7 38 ♗xc4

The threat of ♕c1 mate compels Black to give up the exchange, after which the rest is a simple matter of technique for Kasparov.

38...bxc4 39 ♕xh8 ♖d3

39...♖b7+ 40 ♔a2 ♔c2 41 ♕d4 also wins for White.

40 ♕a8 c3 41 ♕a4+ ♔e1

41...♔d2 42 ♕c2+.

42 f4 f5 43 ♔c1 ♖d2 44 ♕a7 1-0

The game of the century? It's obviously a matter of taste, but this superb effort by Kasparov was voted for by four of the Grandmasters in this book.

What would be your pearl of chess wisdom?

It would be something simple like never give up. You can interpret this as you want, for example never give up on a variation. I think that chess at its most basic is belief in yourself. You have to believe in yourself and never give up!

CHAPTER THREE

Nigel Short

Nigel 'Nosher' Short was born in England in 1965 but now lives in Greece with his wife Rea and their children. He described his career defining moment as becoming an IM at the age of fourteen in Hastings, which made him the youngest holder of the title. I feel compelled at this point to mention Nigel's misguided opinion of women's chess at that age. His assertion that: 'Women will never be great chess players. They just don't have the killer instinct' somehow no longer rings true. I certainly think that Judit Polgar would have something to say about it, particularly since, with her world ranking of 20th, she is five places higher than Nigel!

Nigel was awarded his Grandmaster title in 1984 and put it to great use, winning – among many others – Wijk aan Zee, Hastings and the British Championship. He has been a permanent figure in the World Championship cycle and reached the final in 1993, a match which he lost to Garry Kasparov.

On a final note, if you are ever fortunate enough to play Nigel, always be on your guard and remember his declaration that 'Chess is ruthless: you've got to be prepared to kill people'...

Can you tell me about your chess playing background?
I started playing when I was about five. I saw my dad and elder brother playing and felt an instant attraction to the game and, after a number of months, I started to show some sort of talent.

So, from this point, how did your chess career progress?
As in life, there are sometimes big breakthroughs, similar to a light going on in your head, but most of the time, you chug along and improvements come in small steps.

I played thousands of games as a child, which I strongly recommend. I sometimes look back at my old games and they're not so bad. I recently found some of my old games on *ChessBase*. There's a game that I played against Portisch in a simultaneous when I was nine. I played a couple of reasonable moves and then suddenly had no idea what to do and got into a difficult position. Positionally the guy should have killed me, but I started to play very cleverly, and he allowed me to play some very cunning technical moves, so I escaped.

Why did you choose to become a professional chess player?

Very simply, I was kicked out of school and was basically unemployed. There is absolutely no question in my mind that I would have become a professional anyway and I think that probably, subconsciously, I wanted to be kicked out. I think that I could have been a reasonable something else, a stockbroker or lawyer or something but, on the other hand, it was very clear that my real ability lay in chess. I think that you should always follow up the things you are really good at. Follow your heart.

Who was your chess inspiration?

I have many heroes in chess. If we're talking about early heroes, I very much admire the games of Paul Morphy. His game against the Duke of Brunswick will always be a classic. But I can honestly say that I was not really into Fischer. Maybe his games were a little too complicated and tricky for me at the time, I was only seven, after all. A couple of years later I bought his *My 60 Memorable Games*. This is the sort of book that I have gone back to over the years. For example, I remember when I was preparing for the Biel Interzonal, I reread it then and it was actually very inspirational. I think that such books can be great study aids.

I have also always been very much into Karpov. I know that it's now unfashionable to say such things, but I like Karpov's games very much. He was the world champion when I was becoming a reasonable player and I think that he is one of the world's greatest ever players. I think that my admiration has led me to incorporate some elements of his play in my own style.

So, do you think that in some ways your style of play can somehow reflect your character?

Obviously, some peoples' styles do reflect their character, but I don't think that you can read too much into this. If I think about guys Sir Stuart Milner Barry, he really was incredibly violent in his games; he always played like a caveman. He was also one of the most quiet and gentle guys that I've come across in chess.

There are people who play chess like they are going to the office. They're perfectly happy playing incredibly boring chess all the time; it's just something that they do. Personally, I like to play something with a bit of spark in it. It doesn't necessarily have to be a very attacking game. I'm always equally happy with some fine positional play. Routine, boring chess, that's what I am against.

What do you consider to be your greatest achievement?

My greatest achievement was getting to the World Championship final.

(Unsurprisingly, said with absolutely no hesitation. In February 1993 Short and Kasparov announced the formation of the Professional Chess Association, the PCA. They felt that FIDE had let them down financially, as the World Championship bid that had been accepted was about £1 million short of what was expected. The repercussions were almost instant but affected the chess world for many years. Kasparov was stripped of his FIDE title and they were both dropped from the FIDE rating list.

Short and Kasparov played for the world title in an epic battle, which started on September 6th, 1993 at the Savoy Theatre, London. Although the score-line finished 12½-7½ in Kasparov's favour it was a well-fought and extremely tense match. I would advise anyone eager to learn more about this match and its fascinating history to read The Inner Game, by Dominic Lawson, which offers a compelling insider view of one of the most entertaining and interesting World Championships in our history.

From his privileged position, inside the Short camp, Lawson is able to offer us insights into the mind and preparation of Short, with fantastic details such as: 'On the last weekend before the match Nigel was given a form to fill in by the match managers, asking what he wanted to have provided in his rest room. Under 'special requests' Nigel inscribed in his tiny, neat handwriting, 'Coffee; any sandwiches other than ham; regular massages from Madonna.' On Monday 5th September, the day before the first game, they responded 'Mr Short: Massages from Madonna arranged. Coffee proving a bit more of a problem.')

Another high point of my career was beating Anatoly Karpov. I've won a lot of tournaments in my time, but that was something special.

How do you think that you have improved since your match with Kasparov?

Sadly, I think that I've actually got worse, because I've become very lazy. I don't think that I've got better at all because the evidence all points in the opposite direction.

Are Grandmasters a product of super intelligence or a cultured and trained thought process?

Coaching is very important and intelligence is certainly paramount at the top levels, but not necessarily super intelligence. I think that top quality chess is certainly more to do with a trained thought process.

But how should I train my thought process? Should I and thousands of general tournament players concentrate on improving their openings?

No, no, absolutely not. People should study the games of really strong players. That's what I would recommend. Choose a player whom you really like and try to understand how they play. I think that this is the best way.

If you want to get to the very highest level, then you have to study openings, there is no question about that, but if you want to reach a certain level in chess, try to study a top player's games. If, for example, you have picked someone like Tal, you can actually see how they have developed their opening repertoire.

I see, so do you think that raw talent can only get you so far, after which hard work is the key factor?

To become a great player you have to spend a lot of time studying. I think that one of our main problems in Britain is that there are very few people who know how to study chess properly. I would include myself among them. Matthew Sadler, now there's a guy who knew how to study properly. *(Matthew was notorious for studying over eight hours a day, every day.)*

Thus far, you've mentioned studying Grandmaster games and hard work. What other qualities do we need in order to become great chess players?

What I'll say about myself is that I am capable of raising my game, but I don't always have the energy to play at the highest level. If I really need to move up an extra gear, then I can do it, but I can't manage to do it all the time. I can also effectively motivate myself, which I've proven many, many times, as I'm very good at coming back in situations when I am down in a match. I feel that this is an important strength that not everybody has. Dragging yourself out of the doldrums is one of the toughest things in chess, readjusting your thoughts after a particular game. Because you can't have a history when you are playing a tournament, every game must be a completely separate entity. If you have a bad day, you have to come out very strongly in the next game and most people can't manage to do that. A guy like Kasparov, he never really dwells on his own misery. If he's had a bad day, then the next day he comes out really angry, perfectly ready to tear someone limb from limb.

But can't this type of anger be quite a negative and destructive force?

Well, it depends on how good you are, both at chess and at harnessing your anger!

Another problem that many of us face is the danger of time trouble. How do you personally keep your cool in time trouble?

Well, to be perfectly honest, I don't. I'm very bad in time trouble. If you play a huge amount of chess on the Internet Chess Club (ICC), I think that it is detrimental to your chess in many respects, but in the respect of time trouble it is quite good.

For example, when I played in the Isle of Man a couple of years ago *(1999)* I had a lost position against Psakhis, with 15 moves to make in one minute. I had a lost position, but I was still extremely calm. Maybe it was because I was totally lost. If I had had a slightly better position, then I would have felt the pressure, but in that situation I felt that I had nothing to lose. At this stage he *(Psakhis)* had twenty minutes left on his clock. And I began to launch one tactical blow after another. *(Nigel went on to win the game)* I think that sometimes, with a little bit of practice, it is possible to make a lot of moves in a very short space of time.

How do you see computers affecting the future of chess?

Personally, I absolutely loathe them. Computers mean that some jerk that knows nothing about chess can rattle off dozens of moves of theory without knowing anything about what they are doing. What I don't like about computers is that they can and do make people lazy.

From another point of view, man versus computer matches attract a huge amount of commercial attention. Used in exhibition matches, computers can be of great benefit to the chess world. However, as I have previously said, I oppose the introduction of computers into international competitions. We don't make sprinters run the 100 metres against a Ferrari!

Is fear the enemy? Should you show total respect, but no fear?

I feel that fear is actually a very bad emotion in chess. And it is also sometimes good not to have any respect for the person that you are playing.

What do you think was your worst blunder?

Definitely when I played against Gata Kamsky. When his father threatened to kill me during the match I should have just refused to continue, there and then. I consider that to be my worst blunder.

Rustam was just a psychopath. He had previously been in prison for grievous bodily harm. He was utterly paranoid and just simply the worst thing in chess. I plainly should have refused to play on. If I had been defaulted, then so be it, that would have been it, but I foolishly continued the match.

During the next game, at one particular moment – it was actually quite early on, move fifteen if I remember correctly – I suddenly felt physically exhausted. All my energy had gone. I had been completely sapped of all energy. Strange as it may sound, I'm not used to having homicidal maniacs approach me during chess tournaments and threaten to kill me! This was easily my most unpleasant time, my most unpleasant experience in chess. On a scale of one to ten, if you consider this to be a ten, my next worst episode would have been a two and a half. It was fantastically unpleasant!

On a more pleasant note, what do you consider to be your best game?

I couldn't tell you what my best game ever is, but I can easily tell you my most popular game. Absolutely wherever I've been, whether it's the Galapagos Islands, Mongolia or Ecuador, there have been people who have spoken to me about my game against Timman, Tilburg 1991, which actually won the best game prize in *Chess Informant* for that particular issue. It involves a monumental king march where my king finally arrives on g5.

It was a good game, if a bit one sided. It was not Jan's finest day, although I do think that I played very well. It was an extremely nice trick, especially when I was actually in time trouble. The one thing that detracts from my enjoyment is that when I played 31 ♔h2 he could have played 31...♗c8, compelling me to sacrifice a rook. This variation does win by force, but I was very short of time and I'm not sure that I would have played it and, had I not done so, I probably would have thrown away practically all of my advantage. That is what I know about this game, which in general, people do not know.

Sometimes you see these very nice games, by people like Alekhine and he's said 'Well of course I calculated the following variation.' which is all total rubbish. He hadn't seen any of it, or he saw some of it and he miscalculated the rest and by some miracle he was winning at the end. After my game, if I analyse it as I analysed it in *Chess Informant*, you can see that this was a flawless game by me, but I am not sure that I would have played the right move had he played the most stubborn defence. It is, in fact, most likely that I would not have played the right move, but as it turns out, the result was still the same, a flawless game, a magnificent game.

Short–Timman
Tilburg 1991
Alekhine's Defence

---

1 e4 ♘f6 2 e5 ♘d5 3 d4 d6 4 ♘f3

This is White's most solid and perhaps promising line against the Alekhine's Defence. Rather than go for the obscure complications of something like the Four Pawns Attack, White simply develops a piece.

4...g6

The Alburt Variation. Black intends to pressurise the e5-pawn.

5 ♗c4 ♘b6 6 ♗b3 ♗g7 7 ♕e2

The battle lines are drawn from an early stage. Both sides seek to control the key e5-square.

7...♘c6 8 0-0 0-0

Black would like to continue the fight for e5 with 8...♗g4, but this falls foul of the winning blow 9 ♗xf7+.

9 h3

This is a move that White would like to do without, but ...♗g4 was a real threat.

9...a5 10 a4 dxe5

Black decides to relieve some of the cramp in his position by exchanges. His

other main option is to play the blockading ...d6-d5 at some stage, but this gives up the battle over e5 for good.

11 dxe5 ♘d4 12 ♘xd4 ♕xd4 13 ♖e1 e6

Surrendering in the fight for e5 for the time being as 13...♘d7 was well met by 14 e6! in Minev-Alburt, Romania 1978.

14 ♘d2

Preparing to once again bring the knight to f3 to bolster the e5-pawn.

14...♘d5 15 ♘f3 ♕c5 16 ♕e4

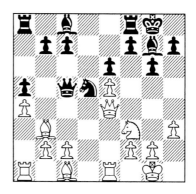

Short begins to manoeuvre with great effect. Black has to be careful that he is not quickly mated by the simple plan of ♕h4, ♗h6 and ♘g5 etc.

16...♕b4

If Black wants to interfere with White's plan he has to do so now, before the rook can join in the fun on e4.

17 ♗c4

Of course Short has no interest in exchanging queens. He also forgoes the chance to win a pawn, the priority being to maintain his grip on the position. 17 ♗xd5 is the greedy move, when Black has active pieces and the bishop pair as compensation after 17...exd5 18 ♕xd5 ♗e6.

17...♘b6 18 b3!?

Another clear sign that White is in a fighting mood. By allowing Black to damage his structure White rules out Black's dream of exchanging queens.

18...♘xc4 19 bxc4 ♖e8

Black has to take time out to defend against the threat of ♗a3.

20 ♖d1

With the e5-pawn securely defended White makes a useful prophylactic move, hindering the development of Black's queen's bishop.

20...♕c5 21 ♕h4

White uses a tactical trick to provide his queen with a more aggressive post on the kingside.

21...b6

The foolhardy 21...♗xe5?? loses a piece to 22 ♗a3.

22 ♗e3 ♕c6

Black aims to keep White's potentially lethal knight fixed on its current square by preparing a battery of queen and bishop along the a8-h1 diagonal.

23 ♗h6 ♗h8

Black must try to preserve his dark-squared bishop, as can be seen from the variation 23...♗xh6 24 ♕xh6 ♗b7 25 ♖d4, when the threat of ♖h4 is impos-

sible to meet.

24 ♖d8!

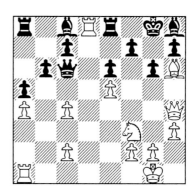

White's stranglehold continues. The threat is ♘d4.

24...♗b7

The natural response, but Black possibly misses his last chance to put up serious resistance.

24...♗d7 is, I believe, a suggestion of John Nunn, who pointed out that after 25 ♘d4 ♖axd8 26 ♘xc6 ♗xc6 Black has chances of saving the game in view of his better pawn structure, and White will find it hard to activate his rook without dropping a pawn.

25 ♖ad1

Now Short is in total control.

25...♗g7

Again greed is not good, as 25...♗xe5 allows 26 ♕e7, which leaves Black defenceless against the threat of ♖xa8 followed by ♖d8.

26 ♖8d7

Short continues to turn the screw, setting some dangerous traps in the process. The threat is the simple ♗xg7 followed by ♕f6+, but there is only one good defence.

26...♖f8

The plausible attempt to exchange

White's most dangerous piece by 26...♕e4 loses horribly to 27 ♖xf7!! ♔xf7 28 ♖d7+ ♔g8 29 ♖xg7+ ♔h8 30 ♕f6 with mate to follow on g7. Meanwhile 26...♘xe5 allows the killer blow 27 ♖xf7!.

27 ♗xg7 ♔xg7 28 ♖1d4

Black's pieces are completely closed out of the game as White decides upon the decisive breakthrough.

28...♖ae8

Black would love to try to evict the rook on d7 but, unfortunately, 28...♗c8 loses immediately to 29 ♕f6+ ♔g8 30 ♖xf7.

29 ♕f6+ ♔g8 30 h4

The plan is simple yet deadly. March the pawn to h6 and deliver mate on g7.

30...h5

30...♗c8, attempting to evict the rook, again fails if White continues thematically with 31 h5 gxh5 32 ♖g4+! hxg4 33 ♖d4, with mate to follow shortly.

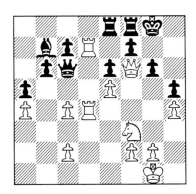

Black has beaten off the first wave of the attack, stopping the h-pawn in its tracks. The question is what is White to do next? All his pieces seem to be in optimal positions, with the exception of the knight, which is limited due to the

mate threat on g2. The answer that Short now comes up with is truly remarkable!

31 ♔h2!! ♖c8

This is the moment that Nigel is talking about. Now really is the time for Jan to try 31...♗c8, when White has to find – despite being very short of time – the winning move, 32 g4! – again, the idea is to march the pawn to h6 to mate on g7. After 32...hxg4 33 ♘g5! ♗xd7 (33...♗b7 34 f3, while 33...g3+ is tricky but White's king is once again the key piece to negotiate victory: 34 ♔xg3 ♗xd7 35 ♔h2, preventing ...♕h1 and preparing h5-h6) 34 h5 gxh5 (34...g3+ 35 fxg3 ♕xa4 36 h6 ♕xc2+ 37 ♖d2 wins as Black cannot avoid mate on g7) 35 ♕h6 the mate on h7 cannot be prevented. The alternatives are less difficult for White to deal with, e.g. 32...♗xd7 33 gxh5 ♔h7 34 ♘g5+ ♔h6 35 ♘xf7+ and wins, or 32...♗b7 33 ♖d3 ♕e4 34 gxh5 ♕f5 35 ♘g5 when Black's problems are far from over.

32 ♔g3

The king continues the long march, which Black is curiously powerless to prevent.

32...♖ce8 33 ♔f4 ♗c8 34 ♔g5 1-0

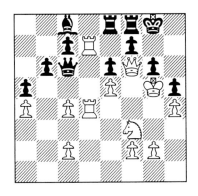

The king is coming to h6 and, as 34...♔h7 loses to both ♖xf7+, Black decides enough is enough. A strategical masterpiece by Nigel.

What do you think is the best game ever played?

Cricket is the best game! *(Nigel is a huge cricket fan and even plays for an amateur team in Greece)...* Oh, yes, I see what you mean. I think chess is too rich a subject just to choose one game.

Okay, then pick a player – you've said how highly you rate Karpov.

Ah ha, yes. I like his game against Unzicker in the Closed Spanish. Karpov is White and he plays ♗a7, a bizarre move. Well, actually it's completely logical, but it's just not the first move that comes into your head.

Karpov-Unzicker
Nice Olympiad 1974
Ruy Lopez

---

1 e4 e5 2 ♘f3 ♘c6 3 ♗b5

The Ruy Lopez has proved to be a loyal servant to Karpov throughout his long and distinguished chess career. There have been very few players who have understood its intricacies so deeply.

3...a6 4 ♗a4 ♘f6 5 0-0 ♗e7 6 ♖e1 b5 7 ♗b3 d6 8 c3 0-0 9 h3 ♘a5

The knight chases the bishop from the dangerous a2-f7 diagonal, thus initiating the Chigorin Defence. Traditionally this has always been one of the most popular ways of meeting the Lopez. Such is Karpov's experience with both colours in this opening that one of the variations now bears his name. The move 9...♘d7 aims to reinforce the e5-pawn and was employed four times by Karpov in his 1990 World Championship Match with Garry Kasparov.

10 ♗c2 c5 11 d4 ♕c7

It is totally understandable why this has been Black's main preference in this position. The queen offers further support to the e5 square and, if White leaves the centre untouched, may provide useful counterplay down the c-file.

12 ♘bd2 ♘c6 13 d5

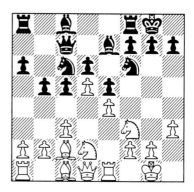

The main problem with the Chigorin Variation is that Black's queen's knight tends to lack a decent square. The rest of Black's position is fine, if slightly passive, but the knight is certainly a problem piece.

13...♘d8 14 a4

White begins his quest to wrest control of the a-file from Black. This serves to nullify any queenside counterplay before White starts attacking on the kingside.

14...♖b8

14...♗b7 is an ugly move which simply misplaces the light-squared bishop.

15 axb5 axb5 16 b4 ♘b7

The knight has moved five times and is still to find somewhere to call home. After this game Black's efforts became concentrated on the move 16...c4 when, after some manoeuvring, the d8-knight can hope to settle on the slightly superior f7-square.

17 ♘f1 ♗d7 18 ♗e3

Karpov has always been very strong in the area of prophylactic play. Here he prepares in advance for Black's plan of counterplay on the open a-file.

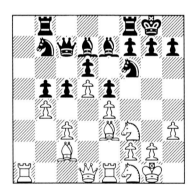

18...♖a8 19 ♕d2 ♖fc8 20 ♗d3

In an effort to lure the c-pawn forward Karpov targets the potentially weak pawn on b5. We'll see why in a few more moves!

20...g6 21 ♘g3 ♗f8 22 ♖a2

Preparing to take control of the a-file by force.

22...c4

The threat of ♖a1 spurs Black into action, but this queenside thrust is no more than a fly in the ointment as far as Karpov is concerned.

23 ♗b1 ♕d8

Black is trying to organise a mass trade on the a-file. If successful this would make the defensive task much easier, but Karpov has other plans.

24 ♗a7!

The star move of the game! White thwarts his opponent's plan of making wholesale exchanges and gives himself plenty of time to pile up the heavy artillery on the a-file.

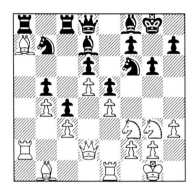

24...♘e8 25 ♗c2 ♘c7 26 ♖ea1

Karpov's plan has worked to perfection. Black must now be constantly on the lookout for a sneaky retreat by White's dark-squared bishop, unleashing an attack against the rook on a8. However, by no means does White have to rush this, whereas Black must be permanently on his guard.

26...♕e7 27 ♗b1 ♗e8 28 ♘e2 ♘d8 29 ♘h2 ♗g7 30 f4

With the queenside in his pocket Karpov, quite naturally, turns his attention to the kingside.

30...f6

30...exf4 31 ♕xf4 opens a diagonal for Black's dark-squared bishop but in return gives White access to the important d4-square. An agonising choice for Black, but at least this pawn trade serves to free his position slightly.

31 f5 g5

Black is doing his best to keep the position closed but, unfortunately for Unzicker, this trench warfare suits Karpov's style.

32 ♗c2

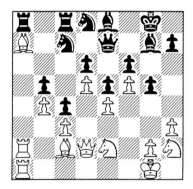

The nice thing about Karpov's play is that he spots what he wants to do and then just goes for it. Here you can almost feel him thinking, 'Hmmm, h5 looks like a good square for one of my pieces. Does Black have any meaningful counterplay? No, I prevented that a long time ago, so let's get on with the business of winning the game...'

32...♗f7 33 ♘g3 ♘b7

33...h5 further weakens the kingside without concerning White too much, e.g. 34 ♗d1 h4 35 ♘h5, when White can open up with g2-g3 at the appropriate moment.

34 ♗d1 h6 35 ♗h5

White clearly wants to occupy the light squares on the kingside and it is standard practice in such situations to first remove potential defenders.

35...♕e8 36 ♕d1 ♘d8 37 ♖a3

Black is powerless, prompting Karpov to tease his opponent, hinting at the possibility of trebling major pieces on the a-file, and leaving Black in no doubt as to who is in control.

37...♔f8 38 ♖1a2 ♔g8 39 ♘g4 ♔f8 40 ♘e3

One by one, Karpov has slightly improved the position of all his pieces before launching the final assault.

40...♔g8 41 ♗xf7+ ♘xf7

41...♕xf7 avoids immediate slaughter but Black cannot be blamed for steering clear of the suffering that follows 42 ♕h5 ♕xh5 43 ♘xh5 ♔f7 (43...♘b7 44 ♘c2, preparing ♗b6, shows why the knight was first redeployed to e3) 44 ♗b6, when the invasion on the a-file will cost him material.

42 ♕h5 ♘d8 43 ♕g6 ♔f8 44 ♘h5 1-0

As we have already seen an exchange of queens does not alter Black's plight and, in any case, the pressure is becoming unbearable and White has his choice of ways to win.

A strategical masterpiece by one of the kings of strategy. Karpov was in complete control of this game from start to finish, giving his opponent no chance. Once Karpov achieves a stranglehold over positions of this nature, expect to be squeezed until your bones crack!

What would be your pearl of wisdom for the chess playing world?

Give up chess and play backgammon! No, no.

Just remember that chess is not an easy game. It is not something that one can learn easily. Hard work is the key.

CHAPTER FOUR

Alexander Khalifman

Alexander Khalifman was born on 18th January 1966 in Leningrad. After learning chess as a child he attended the famous Pioneers' Palace chess school. Winning the Soviet Union's Junior Championships in 1982 and 1984 coincided with the moment that he decided chess was to be his future profession.

Compulsory army service in 1987 halted his chess career, after which he felt that it took him the whole of 1989 to 'wash off the tremendous irritation' that had been accumulated during his army days. However, his breakthrough came in 1990, when qualifying for the Interzonal and winning the New York and Moscow Opens earned him the Grandmaster title, a title that he felt his play had merited for a long time.

Alexander founded the highly regarded Grandmaster Chess School in 1996, but it is his 1999 World Championship victory for which he is most remembered. Alexander entered the championship ranked 45th in the world and 36th of the seeded 100 players in Las Vegas, but emerged as the 14th World Champion. He has described his victory as a dream come true. A modest and quiet man, whenever asked about his Las Vegas victory he would answer: 'I do not claim to be the world's best chess player, but I am the FIDE World Champion, the only championship of the world that we have now.' His title and newly found fame allowed him to meet, among others, the Russian Prime Minister, and to greatly increase publicity for his chess school.

In the years following the Las Vegas championship he continued to play outstanding chess, including a magnificent result at Hoogeveen 2000, where he achieved the highest ever performance rating of 3028 Elo.

At this point I would like to hand you over to his friend and former Leningrad team-mate, Grandmaster Yermolinsky, who phrases this better than I ever could: 'El Khalif never gave the impression of a man on a mission. He never trampled people under his feet, never used anybody, never threw anybody out of his heart because they were no longer needed.

He's lived his life the way he saw fit at that moment, day by day, like we all do. Yes, he's made mistakes, he's done things that he wishes he could take back, so what? It only proves that a human being can win a world title in chess, and it gives us all hope.'

Tell me a little about your chess playing background?

My father showed me the rules of the game when I was about six. And no surprise, I lost some of my first games. Well, well, I guess that I'm no Capablanca, even though my father plays chess better than Capa's father did. After a while my uncle presented me with my first chess book, *Journey to the Chess Kingdom* by Yuri Averbakh and M. Beilin. I have no idea whether this book was ever translated into English, so my title translation might not be the most accurate. It's a guide for kids starting to play chess and, in my opinion, it's one of the very best books of its kind.

After this I became extremely interested in chess and my parents had no choice but to take me to the famous chess school in Leningrad, The Pioneers' Palace, where, for instance Taimanov, Korchnoi and Spassky began their chess careers. *(His first coach was Wassili Byvshev, one of the most successful Soviet Masters of the 1950s)*

Who is, or was, your inspiration?

In different periods I've had different heroes: Alekhine, Tal and Fischer influenced my play the most, although I've carefully studied the games of many great players and I hope that they've helped me to play better.

What was chess life like in Russia in the 1980s, and what is it about St. Petersburg that inspires such great chess players?

Tradition is the right word. Chess was always very popular in Russia and there were many good teachers. Due to the recent social and economic changes the situation is a bit different now, but the tradition still exists.

My city has always been the centre of chess life in Russia, which started in the 19th century with Petrov and Chigorin, so in St. Petersburg the chess tradition is even stronger than in the rest of the country.

How did things change for you when you attained your Grandmaster title in 1990?

In my own life nothing special changed in 1990. I clearly understood that I had played like a Grandmaster for some years, but there were not so many opportunities to play in Grandmaster norm tournaments. So, every time I got such a chance, I was always very nervous and therefore I missed the Grandmaster norm by half a point many times. When I finally got the title I could relax and I made Grandmaster norms in something like ten tournaments in a row.

Could you tell me a little about your chess school?

Well, what can I tell you? It was thinking nostalgically about the Pioneers' Palace, where I studied chess a long time ago, and that pushed me towards organising my own chess school. There are so many good chess coaches in St. Petersburg that I didn't want, and still don't want, to connect the school with my name, so it's just The Grandmaster Chess School.

(The motto of the school is Chess = Intellect + Character) Right now the school has two branches. One is a chess school solely for St. Petersburg kids. Our teachers give lessons in different areas of the city and also in the central office. Right now one of our best guys, IM Evgeny Shaposhnikov, is playing in the World Junior Championships *(Final result – shared 5th in the World Under-20).* But the result that I'm most proud of is that, due to our efforts, hundreds of small kids in St. Petersburg have been able to join the magnificent world of chess.

The second branch is the Internet-based *www.gmchess.com*. In this rather new area of chess education we are also making good progress. We offer a wide range of online and e-mail services and our audience consists of students of very diverse ages from all over the world, from Brazil to Hong Kong. As I don't believe that even the most sophisticated software – at least at the moment – can make online teaching as effective as live analysis with a good coach, we welcome our Internet students to St. Petersburg for some 'live sessions'. Many have already visited our city.

(The intensive chess programme offered by the Grandmaster Chess School includes Grandmaster simultaneous displays, lectures, individual consultations, rapid and blitz tournaments, psychological lectures about memory training, improvement of concentration etc.

Alexander's chess website gmchess.com is one of the best laid out and user-friendly chess websites that I have seen, and I highly recommend that you take the time to look it up. In amongst all the careful detail are such fantastic original touches as their chess quote of the day, for example: 'If drink is the curse of the working classes and work is the curse of the drinking classes, then chess is the curse of the thinking classes.')

This is what Alexander modestly had to say about gmchess.com: Thanks for the high assessment of our efforts, but I'm just rather critical right now. I can see many problems that we have to solve in order to make it one of the best. I hope, actually I'm sure, that we'll be able to improve.

Do you now consider yourself to be a teacher or a professional chess player?

I must admit that I never considered myself to be a teacher. As I have already said, in St. Petersburg there are so many good chess teachers of all profiles. In my city there are some coaches who can be very good for beginners, some for average level students etc. Sometimes I give lectures to students, but not very often, as most of all I try to find the coach who can be the most useful to a certain student, or group of students.

The thing that was really missing from coaching was good management. So when I called myself a 'school director' *(headmaster)* – I don't know if it sounds right in

English – it was really whom I considered and still consider myself to be. I never studied management, that's true, but as I had the understanding and energy and no international level manager was too eager to join the project, I read some books and decided to do the organisation part of the project on my own. Did I do it well or not? Only time will tell.

My result in Las Vegas was a real breakthrough which gained enormous publicity, not only for me, but also for my school. From the autumn of 1999 I decided to combine both activities – 'school director' and 'professional grandmaster', sometimes giving more attention to one and sometimes to the other.

Winning the World Championship must have been phenomenal

It was. The feeling that I had after the final game was incredible. However, rather too soon I was down to earth again, thanks to my numerous critics.

How much of a role did confidence and mental preparation play?

My preparation was nothing special, except that I didn't play chess for sixth months and was really 'hungry' to play. Confidence might be the right word; it was always my strong point. I started to feel very confident at the start and this never left me.

(The press went wild about Alexander's victory in Las Vegas. A quiet, thoughtful and previously little known Russian Grandmaster, rated at that time 45th in the world, had ploughed his way through the ranks of higher profile Grandmasters to become the 14th Chess World Champion. You have heard him say that this victory was due to confidence, but unlike many of the more cautious Grandmasters, he had played aggressive chess and freely admitted that he wasn't afraid to take reasonable risks. The very last game of the championships was a mammoth seven hour tussle in which his opponent, Akopian, actually missed a move that would have forced a draw.)

The following is a short excerpt from the Las Vegas Sun's *account of Alexander at this final match:* 'Alexander Khalifman planted his elbows on the table and eased his cheeks into his palms, the very picture of a man bearing up under the weight of this final round of the World Chess Championship and the Nimzo-Indian Defence forming on the board before him. Then the tap. Not a hard arrogant aggressive tap some chess players prefer after their move. Just a light tap on his clock, to press the button that would start his opponent's clock. And, just like clockwork, his post-move ritual followed. His tall frame, clad in a dark blue suit and light-blue striped open collared shirt, rose from the leather chair until standing straight as a ceremonial soldier. With a solemnity speaking volumes about the seriousness of this 33-year-old Russian Grandmaster, Khalifman clasped his hands behind his back and willed his brown shoes into a glide towards his retreat behind the curtain.

Then, after the game and the Championship were finally won, Alexander met with the press, sharing analysis and laughter. He talked about the history of chess, the problems of previous World Champions and the scandals of old. He mused that the good reputation of chess had suffered because of the behaviour of certain players. The most charming of all his responses came to the question of what he intended to do with his $660,000 winnings: 'I do not know, but my wife is a practical woman and will not spend it all in one month.'

You would think that winning the World Championship would be achievement enough, but Alexander was not content with just one such monumental result. In October 2000 he achieved the highest ever performance rating of 3028. I asked him how he felt about this.

I must admit I was quite happy after the Hoogeveen tournament, but not because of some stupid number, 3028, 15902 or 43, whatever it was. I was just in good shape and did my job quite well. The only thing I was really proud of was that I didn't try to secure first place after the first half of the tournament by making some draws, but I just continued to play some good games of chess. It was not a success, but just another result.

(Such serene responses to questions about extraordinary achievements allude to the nature of Alexander's personality. But it's somehow a relief to know that, even he, despite his calmness, can be distracted by something as massive as being World Champion)

'It was almost like I felt obliged to prove something. Over the board I'm thinking about the position, I see some move, I want to play it, but then I think that this move is nothing special. I'm a World Champion, so I should do something really ingenious. Such stupidity. Here in Hoogeveen I just played as I play, not as world champion, but as Alexander Khalifman' – Hoogeveen tournament website.

In the past you have tried to tackle FIDE about the flaws in the Elo system. Tell me about this?

The existing rating system is full of flaws and I'm able to prove it mathematically, but I don't want to overload this interview with long mathematical formulae.

The 'FIDE boyz' just didn't want to look at my recommendations. I didn't just tackle them once. I have both written and spoken to the FIDE representatives responsible for the rating system. But to seriously discuss any possible changes one has at least to understand what the system is all about. And certainly, it's not unreasonable to expect somebody who is responsible for the FIDE rating system to have at least some basic mathematical knowledge. No way!

The main consequence of this inaccurate system, especially for those in the top 100, is that those who regularly play in round robins are massively overrated in comparison to those who compete in Open tournaments. Once more, I can prove it mathematically, but I'll write down all these formulas when I feel that something might actually change.

Now, moving from the personal to the general, how can computers help with the advancement of chess?

Chess computers are surely very good for chess training, but I don't think that just playing games with computers helps a lot if you're trying to improve. Computers are very good to analyse certain positions, or to check the validity of your own thoughts during a specific game. More sophisticated methods of computer training are still to be worked out.

Online tournaments are certain to be popular in the future. They seem to grab public attention and can have an audience of millions. Such events will develop much more in the next few years.

Does it worry you that chess may be just a puzzle waiting to be solved?

I don't think that computers are a threat to chess, they're just reality. Even if at some moment – not so soon, I guess – the game of chess is 'solved' by some silicon monster, people will still be able to play and will still enjoy the game. The only thing that can be achieved by computers is the knowledge of the best move(s) in any possible position. They will never produce the verbal algorithm 'how to win'.

Do you recommend blitz as a training tool?

First of all it depends on the aims of each individual chess player. For someone who is playing chess just for fun, blitz is quite okay, but for a young improving player, blitz can be a very dangerous drug. Yes, it's just a drug, because the habit of playing hundreds of blitz games a week is not so easy to get rid of.

So blitz can be recommended in very limited portions and for certain purposes. For instance, playing some thematic games to understand the basic ideas of a new opening system. But bullet *(one minute chess)*, this terrible ICC product – never!!! The ICC is a great place where people can play chess and communicate, but not much more.

'Classical chess is the Royal game, which brings us the great ideas and concepts. In my opinion, we must try to protect chess from becoming only fun and entertainment' – *this is, ironically, taken from an ICC chat with Khalifman.*

What are the qualities that make a great chess player?

The answer is easy, although most probably doesn't explain much – it's chess genius. Genius is something man is born with and is hard to define or even describe. Its correlation with some other talents (mathematics, for example) is not necessary. The players who lack this genius can reach some very good results with a lot of work and energy, but their role is rather sad – just to be forgotten. Only the names of geniuses remain in history. Pretty sad, but what to do: our cruel world has always belonged to the Mozarts – not to the Salieris. *(Salieri was a moderately talented composer of the same era as Mozart, but his music was totally overshadowed by Mozart's creative genius. He was rather fancifully credited with having poisoned Mozart)*

Can you pinpoint differences in your play that come with age?

I'm afraid my answer to this question would be rather trivial. The style differences between the age of twenty and thirty-five are quite obvious. The younger player has more energy and a better memory. When one gets older there comes experience, which brings better self-control and good knowledge of psychology (my own and my opponents'). These are the basic differences – I can hardly add something new.

When you look at a chess position what do you see?
Firstly, I look for the forced win. If I fail, then I look for the forced draw. If I still fail, I try to find the best move. The way that I evaluate positions is rather primitive.

'I like watching the game as an analytical problem that always has a solution.' – From a collection of interviews by Atarov.

How do you fix on and confront your greatest weakness?
Sorry, as I'm still a practical player, I wouldn't like to tell everybody (including my possible opponents) about my weaknesses. The only thing I can say about them is that to improve you must clearly understand your weaknesses and try to get rid of them.

What chess book would you recommend?
There have been many good books for all levels and on all aspects of chess. And although some good books continue to appear, right now a lot of junk is regularly coming onto the market. I don't know English chess literature quite so well, so for me, it's hard to recommend something new. If we're talking about classics, my point of view is hardly original, but if I had to name one book, it would be Nimzowitsch's immortal *My System*.

This is one of my favourite questions: Can you explain the psychology of the draw offer?
One of my favourite subjects, as well. After thinking for a long time about this problem I came to some basic and rather primitive conclusions. If you want to improve your play and score good results, there must be no psychology at all!

One has to offer a draw when the position is dead equal and offers no reasonable possibilities for more play. All the rest is wrong! Offering a draw in a worse position is unethical and just shows lack of respect for your opponent. Offering a draw in a better position because of something – tiredness, lack of confidence and so on, is also wrong. If one feels like this, then it's better not to play at all.

How do you define chess?
I don't feel like trying to give a formal definition to chess. Let somebody else do this. I'd better try to explain what, in my opinion, is the value of chess in the modern world. Western civilisation is very comfortable. As one good friend of mine said 'The only skills one needs are to drive a car and to push appropriate buttons.' Thinking is not necessary at all. So, from my point of view, the basic value of chess is that it really makes people think. Even more, this value seems to remain unri-

valled; it does not matter if computers reach perfection in chess, or how soon it happens.

Can you tell me what you consider to be your best game and why?

Quite sincerely, I believe that throughout my career I have played some good games and I even hope to play some more. It's hard to select the 'one and only', but if I have to name one, then let it be the game with Bogdan Lalic from the Linares Open 1997.

This game is, in my opinion, a good one for you to feel the wild spirit of the Benko gambit, one of my favourite openings. It's full of wild tactical complications. However, to play them well one has to feel the positional basis of these positions and to be ready to sacrifice some material just for dynamic positional compensation. So, it's not a perfect opening for the 'silicon monsters'.

This game is a good example of all I've written above. I'm especially proud of the positional move ...h7-h5!, which I found over the board after forty minutes' thought. Once more, about the opening – with all respect to Grandmaster Pal Benko, I like the Russian name Volga Gambit, it just sounds more like *(the character of)* this opening. Playing this gambit is quite often like a 'ride across the river – deep and wide' – Dire Straits.

Lalic-Khalifman
Linares 1997
Benko Gambit

1 d4 ♘f6 2 c4 c5 3 d5 b5

The Benko Gambit is an excellent choice for those players who want to generate winning chances with Black. This game, played at the famous Linares Open tournament, required both players to go for the win, hence Khalifman's choice.

4 cxb5 a6 5 f3

This is one of White's most aggressive tries against the Benko. Lalic aims to quickly build a broad pawn centre and then target Black's somewhat loose structure on the queenside.

5 bxa6 is the main line, when Black uses the open a- and b-files, in conjunction with a kingside fianchetto, to gen-

erate long lasting compensation for the pawn deficit.

5...e6

This is Alexander's most uncompromising choice. He hits out at the advanced pawn on d5 before White is in a position to properly support it. This leads to some of the most fascinating and complicated lines of this tricky gambit.

6 e4 exd5 7 e5

7 exd5 may seem like the most natural move in this position, but after 7...♗d6 White has to be careful not to be murdered on the e-file and/or the weakened dark squares on the kingside. And after 8 ♕e2+ ♔f8 9 ♘c3 axb5 10 ♗e3 c4! 11 ♔f2 ♖a5 12 g3 (which occurred in another of Khalifman's games, when he played against Bareev in the 1995 Russian Championships) Black has the very promising plan of targeting the

weak d-pawn with moves such as ....♗b7 and ...b5-b4.

7...♕e7 8 ♕e2 ♘g8

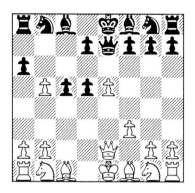

This position looks very odd when you see it for the first time. With both queens obstructing their own bishops it seems as though a couple of beginners have been playing rather than two strong Grandmasters. Appearances are deceptive!

9 ♘c3 ♗b7 10 ♘h3 c4

We can now see a semblance of logic to the odd looking opening sequence. Black seeks counterplay on the queenside to compensate for the weak d5-pawn and congestion on the kingside. Since 1991, when it first appeared in Hertneck's games, this move has become Black's main choice in this sharp line.

11 ♗e3 axb5!

The strongest move, challenging White to recapture.

12 0-0-0

The best response. Lalic ignores material matters for the moment and accelerates development. 12 ♘xb5?! looks natural but allows Black the time to unravel his pieces after 12...♕b4+ 13 ♘c3 ♘e7! 14 a3 ♕a5 15 ♕f2 ♖a6 (in the

Benko Black is always finding creative ways to use his rooks). S.Ivanov-Khalifman, 1997 St.Petersburg Championship, continued 16 ♕d2 ♘f5 17 ♗f2 ♗c5 18 ♖d1 ♗xf2+ 19 ♘xf2 0-0 (as often happens in this variation, if Black can get organised, then White's king and the dark squares weakened by f2-f3 become the most important factor) 20 ♘e2 ♕c7 21 ♕f4 ♘e7 22 ♘g4 ♘g6 23 ♕g3 d6 (naturally ripping open the centre to exploit White's king position) 24 exd6 ♖xd6 25 ♘d4 f5 26 ♘f2 ♘c6 27 ♗e2 ♘xd4 28 ♖xd4 f4 29 ♕g5 ♖e8 30 ♘g4 ♖de6 31 ♖d2 c3 32 bxc3 ♕xc3 0-1. Another impressive performance by Khalifman, showing his mastery of the opening.

12...♕b4

A strange looking move, but also the strongest! With most of his pieces still undeveloped it would appear that Black is hurling his queen into the fray for no apparent purpose. But all will be revealed shortly!

13 ♘f4

Trying to establish a powerful knight on d5. 13 ♖xd5 is another attempt to do so but this is met in a similar way to the game, with 13...♕xc3+ 14 bxc3 ♗xd5, when White's exposed king and Black's solid structure give Black adequate compensation for the slight material deficit.

13...♘e7 14 ♗b6!?

The idea behind this is to cut off squares from Black's queen, but Khalifman has no long-term plans for the future of this piece anyway! 14 ♖xd5 again invites the queen sacrifice 14...♕xc3+ 15 bxc3 ♘xd5, with yet another murky position.

14...h5

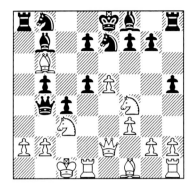

A theoretical novelty at the time, and a strong one. The threat of ...Rh6 forces Lalic to take action, which is, in fact, precisely what Khalifman wants.

15 Rxd5 Wxc3 + !

This, by now, needs no explanation.

16 bxc3 Nxd5 17 Nxd5?!

This natural capture does not make the most of White's tactical opportunities and, as a result, he soon finds himself in a difficult position. More to the point is the pin 17 We4, when Black will most likely have to part with more material in order to obtain sufficient counterplay. After 17...Ra3+ 18 Kd2 Nxb6 19 Wxb7 Bc5 20 Nd5 Rxa2+ 21 Kd1 0-0 22 Nxb6 Bxb6 22 Wxb6 Nc6 Black has only a rook and pawn for queen but retains good compensation as it is very difficult for White to develop the kingside. The situation is then delicately poised, with chances for both sides.

17...Bxd5 18 Wd2

Black's 14th move made the rook swing ..Rh6-a6 possible. The text is directed against this possibility.

18...Be6

18...Bb7 is possible, still allowing the rook swing, but Black's choice is more solid because the bishop now supports the c4-pawn in preparation for the break with ...b5-b4. Additionally the bishop is lined up against the a2-pawn, while on e6 it helps hold up any plans White may have of kingside expansion with f4-f5.

19 Be2

What could be more natural than developing a piece? However, this move fails to take into account Khalifman's effective plan of queenside expansion. White should probably try to exchange off a dangerous attacker with 19 Bc7 Nc6 20 Bd6 Bxd6 21 exd6, when the removal of dark-squared bishops has reduced (but by no means removed) Black's attacking prospects after 21...0-0.

19...Nc6 20 f4

Now there is little alternative to this kingside expansion. 20 Bc7 comes too late as the response is 20...b4 21 Bd6 Bxd6 22 exd6 b3, when the far advanced b-pawn and active queenside pieces give Black a winning position.

20...b4

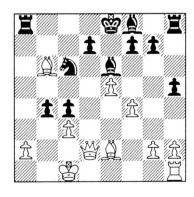

And like lightning, Black strikes!

21 f5

A desperate attempt to deflect Black's bishop. 21 cxb4 ♘xb4 leaves White no way of defending a2.

21...bxc3 22 ♕xc3 ♖a3!

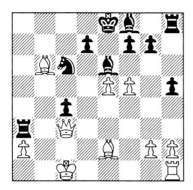

White is given absolutely no breathing space.

23 ♕b2

White had an unappetising choice of possible queen retreats. 23 ♕c2 walks right into trouble in the form of 23...♘b4 24 ♕e4 ♗d5 25 ♕d4 ♘xa2+, when one amusing finale is 26 ♔b1 ♗e4+! 27 ♔a1 ♘c3+ 28 ♔b2 ♖a2+! 29 ♔xc3 ♖c2 mate. Better is 23 ♕a1, but Black is still in control after 23...♗xf5 24 ♗xc4 ♗b4! with the nasty threat of ...♗c3, trapping the queen. Then 25 ♗b3 0-0 followed by bringing the rook swiftly to the c-file and/or ...♗e6 will be very unpleasant for White. 23 ♕e1 is White's best chance, when 23...♗xf5 24 ♗xc4 ♗b4 25 ♕f2 g6 leaves Black with a dangerous initiative but at least White's situation is not as bad as in the game.

23...c3 24 ♕b5

By this stage White has run out of all reasonable alternatives and his choices are limited to simply which way to lose. 24 ♕c2 ♘b4 and 24 ♕b1 ♗xa2 25 ♕e4 ♗b3 are decisive.

24...♗xf5 25 ♖f1 ♖xa2!

The whole game has been played very energetically by Khalifman.

26 ♖xf5 ♘b4

The threat of ...♖a1 mate is very hard to meet.

27 ♕a5

27 ♗d3 is the only way to continue the agony, when 27...♖a1+ 28 ♗b1 c2 29 ♕xb4 ♗xb4 30 ♔xc2 ♖h6 leaves Black an exchange and a pawn to the good, with a technically won endgame. Now White loses at once.

27...g6! 0-1

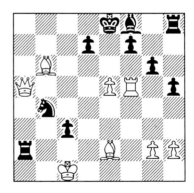

A surprising finish to a masterful attack. The threat of ...♗h6 decides.

And what you consider to be the best game ever played?

Once again this question is too difficult to answer. There were so many good players and they played so many good games. To name one, undeservedly forgotten and most probably less known, I'd like to offer you the black win of the great chess player Isaak Boleslavsky, against another forgotten star Alexander Tolush, played in

Moscow in 1945. The wildness of this game attracted me when I was very young and, even now, I see it as one of the great examples of dynamic attacking chess.

(Grandmaster Isaak Boleslavsky was born in 1919. He played in the U.S.S.R. Championships from 1940-1961, coming second twice. Achievements like this may not sound extraordinary until you remember that these championships were the hunting ground of great players such as Botvinnik and Tal. Boleslavsky was also the coach of the famous World Champion Petrosian. His chess connections also bridged a generation, as his daughter Tatjana married Grandmaster David Bronstein.

Grandmaster Alexander Tolush was also from this well documented era. He is credited with developing crucial King's Gambit theory and was Spassky's trainer. He also fell foul of the geniuses of his age, losing a vital game to Tal in the last round of the 1957 Soviet Championship.)

Tolush-Boleslavsky
Moscow 1945
Trompovsky Attack

---

1 d4 ♘f6 2 ♗g5 c5 3 dxc5

The Trompovsky in its pre-Hodgson era was a very undeveloped surprise weapon. Today both 3 d5 and 3 ♗xf6 (the main line) are more popular.

3...♘e4 4 ♗f4 ♘c6

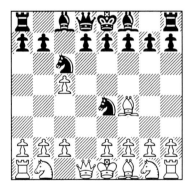

At first sight this move appears to be a mistake, denying Black the opportunity to win back the pawn, but in reality Boleslavsky has seen deeply into the position and is luring his opponent in. 4...e6 is the safe alternative.

5 ♕d5

There is no doubt that Black has a very comfortable type of Sicilian position after 5 ♘d2 ♘xc5 6 ♘gf3 g6 but, nonetheless, this is the more prudent course for White.

5...f5!

Having started on this aggressive course of action Black must continue with it. 5...♕a5+ is asking for trouble after 6 c3, with b2-b4 to follow.

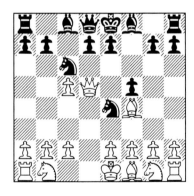

6 ♕xf5

The only consistent follow up to his previous move, as otherwise ...e7-e6 is coming with tempo. Chekhov analysed the following entertaining alternative: 6 f3 e6 7 ♕d1 e5! (not the most obvious move, but a very effective one) 8 ♗e3 ♕h4+ 9 g3 ♘xg3 10 ♗f2 ♕b4+ 11 c3 ♕xb2 12 hxg3 ♕xa1, when Black has a decisive material advantage.

6...d5

White has won a pawn, but at a high price. His queen is being chased around, thus accelerating Black's development.

7 ♕h5+ g6 8 ♕h4

8 ♕f3 is no improvement because after 8...♗g7 Black's ideas of ...♘d4, ...♘e5 and ...0-0 provide more than enough compensation for the material deficit.

8...♘d4

White begins to miss the presence of the queen on the queenside.

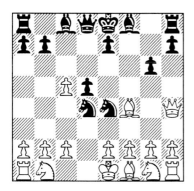

9 ♗e5

9 ♘a3 invites 9...♘f5!, and White's queen is running out of breathing space.

9...♘xc2+ 10 ♔d1 ♘xa1 11 ♗xh8

For the moment White is maintaining his slender material lead, but his problems are just beginning.

11...♕a5

One can hardly blame Black for pursuing White's vulnerable king, and this tactic does indeed prove good enough to win. However, there is a simpler method available in the shape of 11...e5,

after which White has enormous difficulty hanging onto f2 or generating serious counterplay – 12 ♕xh7 ♕g5 and ...♘f2+ is unstoppable.

12 ♘c3 ♘xc3+ 13 ♗xc3 ♕xa2

White's king is in serious trouble.

14 e3 ♕b1+ 15 ♔e2 d4!

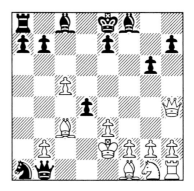

Black rips open the centre in order to further expose the enemy king. However, it is still not too late for Black to go horribly wrong with 15...♗d7 16 ♘h3 ♗b5+? (16...d4!) 17 ♔f3 ♗xf1 18 ♖xf1! ♕xf1 19 ♕a4+

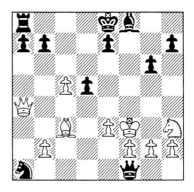

Now, suddenly, the boot is on the other foot.

Returning to the position after 15...d4:

16 ♕xd4

16 ♗xd4 ♗d7 17 ♘h3 ♗b5+ 18 ♔f3 ♗xf1 gives Black a decisive material lead, while 16 exd4 ♗d7 is equally unpleasant for White.

16...♗d7 17 ♕b4

The plausible 17 ♘h3 is met forcefully with 17...0-0-0, and if the queen then decides to flee from the danger zone with 18 ♕h4 Black can finish the game nicely with the spectacular 18...♕d1+! 19 ♔xd1 ♗g4+ with ...♖d1 mate to follow.

17...0-0-0 18 f4

White must provide an escape route for his king.

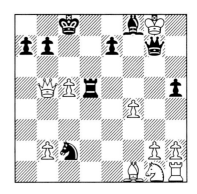

20...♘xd4+

20...♗b5+ 21 ♕xb5 ♖xd4 is also very powerful.

21 exd4 ♕xb2+

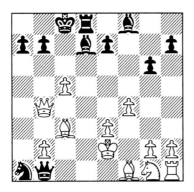

18...♘c2

But sadly, there is no escape!

19 ♕a5 ♕c1 20 ♗d4

20 ♗d2 allows a phenomenal king hunt, starting with 20...♗b5+! 21 ♕xb5 ♕xd2+ 22 ♔f3 ♕xe3+ 23 ♔g4 h5+, when the king is driven to its doom. An amusing finish is 24 ♔g5 ♖d5+ 25 ♔xg6 ♕e6+ 26 ♔h7 ♕h6+ 27 ♔g8 ♕g7 mate.

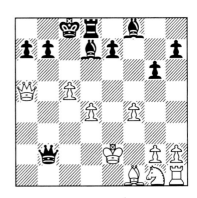

White's king is hopelessly exposed and, with material equality restored, the result is no longer in any doubt.

22 ♔f3 ♕xd4 23 ♘e2 ♗c6+

Ouch!

24 ♔g4 h5+ 25 ♔h4 ♕f6+ 26 ♔g3 e5 0-1

A superbly played attacking masterpiece by Boleslavsky.

What would be your pearl of wisdom for the chess playing community?

Never play for the win, never play for the draw, just play chess!

CHAPTER FIVE

Joel Lautier

Joel Lautier was born 12th April 1973. He and his family moved from Canada to France when he was three and soon Joel started to play chess. His enormous appetite for success led to him quickly becoming the best in his age group, his big breakthrough coming in 1988, when he became the youngest person ever to win the World Junior Championship.

In 1990 he became a Grandmaster and decided to leave school in order to further pursue his chess career, a decision which does not in any way appear to have held back this intelligent, eloquent and multi-lingual man. In 1994 he met his future wife, Woman Grandmaster Elmira (more commonly spelt Almira) Skripchenko. Now rated 2675 Elo, he has made his ambition of entering the world's top ten well known.

Can you tell me about your chess playing background?
My mother taught me how to play chess when I was about four years old. Obviously, I don't remember much about that time, but that's what she tells me. My first recollection of chess was when my father came home and showed me a chessboard and taught me the names of the squares by heart. He just bought me a chessboard without any co-ordinates on it, pointed to some squares and said: which square is this one, and this one. This was my first lesson in blindfold chess, if you can call it that.

I liked chess very much from the start and I played a lot with my parents. First with my mother; we had some long matches *(from the stress that Joel placed on long I gathered that these games would go on for weeks rather than hours)*. Actually, it was quite funny, because my father would prepare me before the game, so I was already sort of a professional by the age of five. I don't think that it matters at what age you learn, whether it's three, four, whatever, but later than seven is a bit late because by that time the mind is already formed in many ways. If you are going to learn chess later on, it will be a little more difficult because, for instance, to play blindfold chess you have to have a very good grasp of the board and, the earlier you start, the better.

After this I started playing among kids and I had some success, which encouraged me to continue. My main advantage in those years in France was that chess was virtually non-existent. We had very few good players – well, none, to be quite honest. I was one of the few kids who started so early and so seriously.

In that situation did the lack of competition make it easier or harder to improve?

Well, in a way it was difficult, but it was also easy because I won everything. So, it made it very exciting for me. Since I was quite quickly the best player for my age, I was able to travel abroad, to the world championships, to play among kids of my age, which was a very good incentive to continue. Of course, after a while you attain a natural level, which you can reach without any help. Then it is more difficult because you need to start looking for stronger players and we didn't have many in France.

My father is a decent player and he was my first coach. His level is about 2200, which was very respectable in those years in France. After that my first real coach was an International Master by the name of Didier Sellos. He was also a decent player *(now rated 2385)*, we played many training games and he accompanied me to some tournaments, which was a big help to me. After that, I was able to meet some of the Grandmasters who came to Paris.

I had a breakthrough result in 1988, when I was fifteen. I became world junior champion, I am the youngest to have won that competition and this opened many doors for me. The immediate effect was that I became quite well known in France and I had a lot of support, which eventually allowed me to get sponsorship from a real estate company. This was very important for the further development of my career – the company's name is Immopar, actually. Of course, I no longer have a contract with them so I don't have to mention them, but just out of gratitude I think that I really should. So I was able to work with Korchnoi, a few training sessions around the age of sixteen, and afterwards with Lev Polugaevsky.

Jumping forward to last year's Brain Games Championships. What was it like working with the world championship team that defeated Kasparov?

Working with Vladimir *(Kramnik)* was an experience that was of enormous benefit to me. I was once his helper before, in 1994; I helped him play his match against Gelfand. Since then we've been very good friends. We've worked together, maybe not on a regular basis, but once in a while, maybe twice a year. So we've always been very close. But working inside a world championship match is a totally different story. That was very hard, of course. But I think that it gave me a lot.

Not only were you part of the team that dethroned Garry, you also previously held the accolade of being the only world-class player with a plus score against him. How did that feel?

Well, Vladimir has joined me now, but it certainly felt very good. That's one achievement that nobody can take away from me.

So, under these circumstances, how is your relationship with Kasparov?

I wouldn't know how to describe it; it's not much of a relationship.

Was being part of the world championship team as exciting as playing for France in the Olympiads?

Playing for France used to be very dull because we were never playing for the top spot. But other than that the Olympiad is fantastic. Actually, we used to have a very nice team, so it was a great atmosphere. It is something that everybody should experience once in their lifetime, because it's a very exciting place to be. I certainly can't complain about the Olympiads, because they allowed me to meet my wife in 1994. *(WGM Elmira Skripchenko-Lautier was born in Moldova in 1976. A talented player with an Elo of 2450, she is the present European women's champion and a former world under-16 champion)*

Do you play much chess at home together?

Yes, we do play, but nothing very serious, we sometimes play blitz games. We don't really train together now. I can certainly say that playing chess too often with your husband or wife can lead to some problems.

You've achieved a great deal in your relatively short chess career, but what achievement is at the top of your wish list?

I would like to – actually it's more than liking – I'm really aiming to reach the top ten in the world. I know that it's a very difficult task, but I still believe that I can achieve it. That is my main objective. When I get there, then I will think about whether I can go further, but let's do that first.

How important do you consider self-belief? And how can you maintain this belief in the face of adverse circumstances?

It's a tricky question, because you could say that the best approach would be to ignore that *(belief in yourself)* and simply get on with the chess variations, with the analysis of the position. But, on the other hand, when you are unsure of yourself you tend to check too many lines too often, to take too much time. I think that it's a question of getting into the rhythm of the game. It sounds a bit like a musical approach, but that's the way I feel it. Sometimes when you are in good shape you can just feel which are the right moments to stop and think and also those moments when you just have to play by hand, as we say.

You just have to trust your intuition because you know that if you are going to work too long on a position you won't come up with a solution that really fits and you will have lost a lot of time in the process.

Khalifman has previously said that chess is an analytical problem that always has a solution. Do you agree, and what is your approach to chess?

I can't really agree. In the absolute sense it's possible *(to always find a solution)* but it would take months to analyse any given position. We have to understand that chess has a different definition for different people. For a composer of chess problems chess is just art, right? Let's say for a trainer it's more of a science, where they have to try and find the best possible move in every position. For a Grandmaster it's a sport. First and foremost, it's a competition.

In my case, since I am more of a competitor than anything else, I would say that most of all, chess is a fight. That is what I really enjoy about the game.

You obviously love many aspects of the game. Do you think that there will come a time when this love fades?

These times do come every once in a while, after you have a bad period, because that's the real mystery of the game. Even though you have reached a different level, you still have moments when you think that you don't understand anything. There are some moments when you seem to do everything possible, you work hard at the board and at home, but you still can't come up with the real ideas, the ones that will truly bother your opponent. And at other times, you don't do anything special at all and everything just comes very easily.

So how do you motivate yourself again and once more fall in love with such a fickle game?

The appeal of victory is such to me that I never stay too long in a bad mood. Motivation is a problem for many players, because the game is very tough and it's like any competition in the sense that you always have to ask yourself questions that are annoying, like why don't you make more progress, why do you keep making this and that mistake. This is quite tough, because in a normal job you can take many things for granted, while in chess it doesn't work that way.

I've read that you are quite keen on analysing your opponents. Does this psychological approach help your play?

It can be a double-edged sword because when you think too much about your opponent you might forget about playing good moves as well. I think that it's good to have a little bit of psychology sometimes. It's more concerning tournament situations, knowing whether your opponent is in a solid or aggressive mood and acting accordingly, because the player himself is quite changeable. He might be willing to attack one day and then, the next, for reasons that you might not know about, he might be in a totally different frame of mind.

Do you consider yourself to be a chess fanatic or a chess professional?

I primarily consider myself to be a chess professional, as everything in my work is geared towards competition. But I'm obviously very fond of the game and I've spent countless hours searching for 'truth' or 'beauty' for the sake of it. As the great French actor Louis Jouvet used to say to his students when he gave acting classes, 'One should put more life in one's art and more art in one's life.'

Do you think that blitz and blindfold chess are a good method of improving your chess skills?

First of all, it really depends on your level. For example if you're a beginner, it doesn't make any sense to study difficult subjects, you first have to get a grasp of the basic things. I think that reading a lot of good books is necessary to start improving your chess. After that, it's essential that you build an opening repertoire. You have to do this in a way that you will feel responsible for your choices, meaning that you will really uphold your lines. Even if you get into trouble, don't immediately switch to something else, but try to find a solution, because switching will make it much tougher for your further career. I think that it's very important to be able to stick to your choices. It helps you to develop a feel for analysis, or rather a taste for it, because if you have some problems to solve, then such analysis will get you used to solving problems. Again, this will be a great help, as you won't try to find a loophole, you will really try to solve your problems.

Later, when you reach a high level, around Master or Grandmaster, you will, unfortunately, have to work a lot on openings. Once you reach a certain level it doesn't matter if you play much better than your opponent in other parts of the game. You have to get a good position out of the opening.

Why do you say *unfortunately*?

Well, the opening comes before the rest – it's a chain of sequences. If you can't get out of the opening then you're dead. But the main attraction of the game to me is not the opening. There are other parts of the game which are just as interesting, the middle and endgame. But these are areas of the game that, even at my level, we don't work on much because we simply run out of time. The opening just takes everything. I think that it is generally very useful to study endgames, for example. We *(Grandmasters)* obviously have extensive knowledge about them, but many Grandmasters have stopped working on these areas of their game because after a while it's not very practical.

If you could ask any chess player, from any period of time, any question, what would it be?

(Joel's almost immediate answer was delivered with great irony)

I think that I would ask Bobby Fischer what is the refutation of the Najdorf! *(Joel has been a huge fan of Bobby Fischer for many years and has described him as the ultimate chess professional)*

Are chess computers only a handicap to those who don't work hard enough?

I think that at the moment you simply can't do without chess computers and this will certainly increase in the future. You have to use them all the time. But I think that they also present a major danger for many players in that they tend to become very lazy. Meaning that if you simply switch on your computer, you stop making your brain work. The main danger for professional players is that the computer tends to replace player judgement. When you analyse an opening, for example, you don't have too much time to spend on a line, you don't have a month, you just have a couple of days, so of course you will use the analysis module *(on ChessBase)* all the time, because otherwise you are being too slow. I think that it's extremely important at some stage to be able to switch your computer off and think for yourself.

(Excerpt of an interview taken from msoworld.com)
'I think that the Net has completed the computer revolution in the chess world. It has made the task of a chess professional so much easier but, on the other hand, it has raised the stakes considerably as far as the opening preparation is concerned.

Nowadays there is no way you can hope to use a devastating novelty, carefully prepared after weeks of hard work, more than once! For all you know, the next potential victim it might have been intended for could be watching your game live via the Net. The appearance of the Net and the immediate availability of any valuable chess knowledge has forced professionals to reassess their preparation techniques.')

What's your opinion of the man versus machine tournaments?

Well, I'm not a big fan of them, simply because it's not really chess. Chess is a fight and these matches are not really an even fight. You have a man, with all the problems that he has, and a machine that is never affected by any external circumstances. These matches are not something that excites me very much but, on the other hand, it's one of the few fields where the best man can still compete with the best machine. So, for the moment, it's still interesting.

(The following excerpt, from a previous interview with Joel (msoworld.com, 12th June 2000), sums up his feelings about both man verses machine tournaments and Kasparov.)
'In 1997, Kasparov lost to a machine clearly weaker than himself, and together with his disgraceful attitude after the match, this has done more harm to the chess world than we could possibly imagine. I believe that the chess professionals should sue him in court for his 7...h6??? in the sixth game, together with the shameful declarations he made at the press conference.

In my mind, there isn't a shadow of a doubt that Kasparov psyched himself out to such an extent during that match that anything playing chess and resembling a tin can would have won that fatal sixth game. The result was a dramatic fall of interest towards chess from the general public and, as an immediate consequence, very scarce sponsorship from private sources.'

(Some of you may not have seen Garry's comments after the historic Deep Blue match, so I've searched high and low on the Internet to find a transcript of the press conference, and below are some of the 'shameful declarations' to which Joel refers.)

'I have my doubts that it was a machine. Some of the machine's decisions cannot be reproduced in pure conditions. The point is that humans can and do make unpredictable moves, but a computer's can be precisely accounted for and should be repeatable, as in a scientific experiment. To prove the success of your experiment you have to be able to repeat it in pure conditions.

The event was organised by IBM, run by IBM, paid for by IBM. Their refusal to release printouts, their refusal to continue with the programme, their decision to dismantle Deep Blue – the only impartial witness – just puts this single experiment out of the scientific rank. So, I think that IBM didn't behave properly, but it's a big corporation and it's virtually impossible to challenge them in the media.'

What are your best and worst chess playing moments?

Let's see. I guess that this will not come as a big surprise, but I would certainly take the first day that I beat Garry, Linares 1994. And also the day that I became world junior champion, that was special.

The worst ones. Oh, it's terrible that you force me to remember this. The worst one might have been in Groningen 1995. I lost something like three games in a row at the end of the tournament. Well, I was totally disgusted with myself, with chess, with everything. I have to admit that I was really depressed and it took quite a few days to recover from that one. It was also something like minus ten Celsius in Groningen; the whole world was against me that day.

I have been asked for an example of Grandmaster humour, can you tell me a joke or a story? The rather strict limitations being that the joke must get approval from the editor.

This is a tricky one, as the best jokes I've heard have been either dirty or plain revolting. Anyway, I've come up with two, so pick whichever you like best.

(This is the one that made me chuckle the most)

A surgeon visits his patient, lying in bed:

'I've got good news and bad news, what shall I start with?' asks the doctor.

'Please tell me the bad news first.' Says the patient.

'Well, the operation failed horribly and we were forced to amputate both of your legs.'

'What good news could you possibly have after that?' asks the shocked and horrified patient.

'Well, the man in the next bed wants to buy your shoes!'

What do you consider to be the best game that you have played?

It's very difficult to make a choice, as some games that I have played are not necessarily spectacular and might leave the reader a little perplexed. I've eventually chosen for you my game against Shirov (with Black) from Dos Hermanas 1995. It's definitely one of the games that brought me the most creative pleasure; it even prompted my friend Alberto David, who acted as my second in that tournament, to ask me for an autograph right after the game!

Shirov-Lautier
Dos Hermanas 1995
Ruy Lopez

---

1 e4 e5 2 ♘f3 ♘c6 3 ♗b5 a6 4 ♗a4 d6 5 c3 ♗d7

Joel sensibly steers clear of the more tactical variations that follow the ambitious 5...f5, which would suit Shirov's creative attacking style.

6 d4 ♘ge7 7 0-0 ♘g6 8 d5

Black has successfully made a stronghold of the e5-square, so it makes sense to gain some space.

8...♘b8 9 ♗c2

Not the most consistent follow-up. With his pawns predominantly on light squares it seems natural that White would want to retain the option of trading light-squared bishops. 9 c4 is logical, preparing a queenside pawn storm. Then 9...♗e7 10 ♘c3 0-0 11 ♗xd7 ♘xd7 12 ♕c2 ♘h4 13 ♘xh4 ♗xh4 14 b4 ♗g5 15 ♖b1 ♗xc1 16 ♖fxc1 ♕e7 gave White a definite pull, thanks to his queenside space advantage, as in the game Van der Wiel-Short, Amsterdam 1991.

9...♗e7

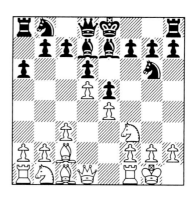

10 h3

Shirov manages to restrict the movement of Black's light-squared bishop, but this comes at a price in the weakening of the dark squares around his king. This may not seem too relevant, but if, for example, a black knight could successfully arrive on f4, it would now be much harder to remove. 10 c4, again with the intention of queenside expansion, is a perfectly decent alternative.

10...h6

Lautier immediately addresses the drawbacks of White's previous move, preparing to occupy f4.

11 c4 &g5 12 ♘bd2

12 ♘xg5?! against an attacking player of Lautier's calibre would be suicidal – 12...hxg5 13 ♘d2 ♘f4, when the storm clouds gather ominously over White's king.

12...a5

Preparing to activate his last minor piece.

13 b3 ♘a6 14 a3 ♘c5

This position reminds me of a Petrosian King's Indian. White has the simple plan of forcing through b3-b4 but, thanks to his active dark-squared bishop, Black can prepare meaningful counterplay on the kingside.

15 ♖b1 ♘f4 16 ♘e1

White has to defend against the threat of ...♘cd3.

16...0-0 17 b4

Finally! White's queenside play gets underway.

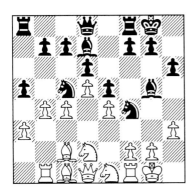

17...axb4 18 axb4 ♘a4

The natural retort. Instead of retreating the knight leaps forward, setting a rather nasty trap in the process.

19 ♖b3

The best way of dealing with the threat of ...♘c3. 19 ♖a1?? falls in with Black's diabolical plan of 19...♘c3 20

♖xa8 ♘fe2+ 21 ♔h1 ♕xa8, when White's queen is trapped on its starting square!

19...b5

Black strikes quickly on the queenside, before he is forced on the defensive.

20 ♖a3

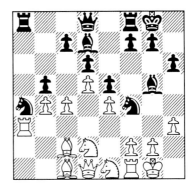

20...bxc4

This tricky move is difficult to resist but preferable might be the more mundane 20...♕e8 21 ♗xa4 ♖xa4 22 ♖xa4 bxa4 23 ♘ef3 f5 with an advantage in view of the mounting pressure on the kingside.

21 h4!

Shirov shows he is up to the defensive task, fighting back on the kingside. 21 ♗xa4 is complicated but better for Black after 21...♗xa4 22 ♖xa4 ♖xa4 23 ♕xa4 ♘e2+ 24 ♔h1 ♘xc1 25 ♘xc4 f5, when Black enjoys the better pawn structure and the more active pieces.

21...♗e7

Practically forced as 21...♗xh4? loses material to 22 g3, when Black cannot save all three attacked pieces.

22 g3

22 ♘xc4 loses material to 22...♗b5 23 ♗xf4 ♗xc4 24 ♘d3 ♘b2.

22...♘h3+ 23 ♔g2 ♘b6 24 ♖c3

Again the most accurate defence. 24 ♖xa8 leaves Black in the driving seat after 24...♕xa8 25 ♖h1 ♕c8 26 ♗b2 c6 27 dxc6 ♕xc6 when, although Black's knight may be a little stranded, White has no obvious way of exploiting this, and Black is a comfortable pawn to the good.

24...♕c8 25 ♖h1

25 ♘xc4?, as before, walks into ...♗b5 after 25...♘xc4 26 ♖xc4 ♗b5.

25...♖a1

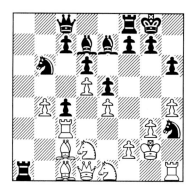

26 ♘xc4?

Shirov finally cracks. The desire to regain the pawn deficit is understandable but, unfortunately, this brings his rook to a vulnerable square. 26 ♗b1 is probably White's best chance, with the intention of ♘c2-e3-f5. This doesn't rule out the tactical strike 26...♗xh4 but it does make it less potent. Then 27 gxh4 is asking for trouble, with 27...♘f4+ 28 ♔g1 ♘a4 29 ♖xc4 ♗b5 giving Black both a powerful attack and some material. We are left with 27 ♘c2 (the point), forcing the rook to make a decision before taking the bishop – 27...♖xb1 28 ♘xb1 ♗e7 29 ♘ba3 ♘g5 30 ♗xg5 ♗xg5 31 ♘xc4 ♘xc4 32 ♖xc4

f5 gives Black, who enjoys the bishop pair and an extra pawn, full compensation for the exchange sacrifice, but there is still plenty of play in the position.

26...♘xc4 27 ♖xc4

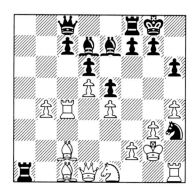

27...♗xh4!

Clearly Black needs to get his knight out of trouble at some point, but most mortals would have tried ...g5-g4 to achieve this.

28 f4

A desperate attempt to deny Black's knight the f4-square. 28 gxh4, as you might expect, leads to trouble after 28...♘f4+ 29 ♔h2 ♗b5, when White suffers due to the poor placement of his rook. Note that here 29 ♔f1 ♗h3+ 30 ♔g1 ♖xc1 wins for Black due to the fork on e2, while 29 ♔g1 ♖xc1 and 29 ♔g3 ♖xc1 30 ♕xc1 ♘e2+ are similar.

28...♗xg3!

Lautier goes for it! The exposed position of White's king and his uncoordinated pieces allow this tactical blow to succeed. 28...exf4? is what Shirov was hoping for, when 29 gxh4 ♗g4 30 ♕d2 gives White good chances of survival.

29 ♔xg3

There are no good alternatives.

29...♘xf4

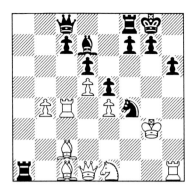

The result of the fine piece sacrifice is that Black – for the moment, at least – has regained control of the important attacking post on f4. The immediate threat is ...♖xc1.

30 ♖h2

Not best, but White is under intense pressure at this stage. After the more accurate 30 ♘d3 Black might open another attacking front with 30...f5 31 ♘xf4 exf4+ 32 ♔g2 fxe4 33 ♗xe4 (33 ♖xe4 ♖a2) 33...♖a2+ with a very strong attack. The main ideas are ...♗b5-e2, allowing Black's queen a route to g4, and ...♗a4.

30...♗b5 31 ♖c3

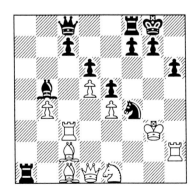

31...♕d8

Black can already win back material,

but sensibly – and in a rather more bloodthirsty fashion – he decides to go for the kill. 31...♘e2+ is the materialistic way to win – 32 ♖xe2 ♗xe2 33 ♕xe2 ♖xc1, and with three pawns and a rook for two pieces Black should win, but there is still considerable technical work to be done.

32 ♕d2 ♕g5+ 33 ♔f3

33 ♔f2 sets up another knight fork with 33...♖xc1! 34 ♕xc1 ♘h3+ 35 ♖hxh3 ♕xc1, winning.

33...♕g1 34 ♗d1

Defending against the threat of ...♖xc1, which overworks White's queen. 34 ♖f2 f5 35 exf5 ♕h1+ 36 ♘g2 ♕h3+ 37 ♔e4 ♕xf5+ is winning for Black.

34...f5

Ripping open another avenue of attack.

35 ♖xc7

35 exf5 allows the following pretty finish: 35...♘d3! 36 ♘xd3 ♖xf5+ 37 ♔e4 ♕d4+ 38 ♔xf5 ♗d7+ 39 ♔g6 ♕e4+ 40 ♔h5 ♗e8 mate.

35...fxe4+ 36 ♔xe4

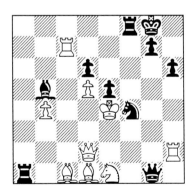

36...♗e8

A nice switchback, hitting the king from another angle.

37 ♖f2 ♗g6+ 38 ♔e3 ♘h3 39 ♘f3 ♕g3 40 ♖g2

Walking into mate, but alternatives serve only to prolong the suffering.

40...♕f4+ 41 ♔e2 0-1

Shirov resigns not wanting to see ...♕xf3+ and ...♕f1+ mate. A wonderful attacking performance from Lautier.

What is the best game ever played?

My all-time favourite game is Nezhmetdinov-Polugaevsky, Sochi 1961, with a very close follower being Kasparov-Topalov, Wijk aan Zee 1999 *(sorry Joel, you're way too late on this one).*

Nezmetdinov-Polugayevsky
Sochi 1961
Sicilian Defence

---

1 e4 c5 2 ♘f3 d6 3 d4 cxd4 4 ♘xd4 ♘f6 5 ♘c3 a6 6 ♗g5 e6 7 f4 b5

This is the brainchild of Polugaevsky, now named after him. Black ignores the pin on his knight in order to initiate immediate queenside counterplay. This leads to some of the sharpest and most complicated lines in the whole of the Sicilian. Not a good choice for the faint-hearted.

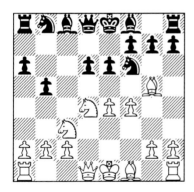

8 e5

While simple development is quite plausible the text has to be the acid test of the variation. White quickens the pace of the game and attempts to exploit the pin on Black's knight.

8...dxe5 9 fxe5

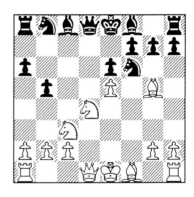

9...♕c7

The point of the entire variation. Black avoids losing a piece by tactical means. 9...h6 10 ♗h4 g5 is the other way of dealing with White's threat, but then both 11 ♗g3 and 11 exf6 gxh4 12 ♕f3 ♖a7 13 0-0-0 are known to give White a good game due to Black's compromised kingside.

10 exf6

10 ♕e2, which momentarily defends the e5-pawn in order to force the knight to flee, is the other main variation here. After 10...♘fd7 White is practically compelled to sacrifice the e-pawn anyway, but hopes that his lead in development will provide compensation.

10...♕e5+ 11 ♘e4

An unnatural looking way of blocking the check, but the only move if White wants to preserve his dark-squared bishop.

11...♕xe4+ 12 ♘e2

12 ♗e2 ♕xg2 13 ♗f3 ♕xg5 14 ♗xa8 ♕h4+ 15 ♔e2 ♕xf6 gives Black very good compensation for the loss of the exchange.

12...♘c6 13 ♕d2 h6!

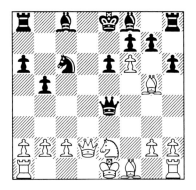

An important move. One of Black's prime concerns is that he may be mated on the d8-square. Therefore, at this point, chasing away the bishop is the most prudent course.

14 ♗e3 ♗b7 15 ♘g3

The preservation of White's dark-squared bishop has come at a price. He has fallen behind in development, a matter that the text seeks to address. 15 0-0-0 ♖d8 is very comfortable for Black.

15...♕e5 16 fxg7 ♗xg7

White has managed to retain material parity, but this is no cause for celebration. Despite White's slight structural superiority it is Black who has won the opening battle, with his two raking bishops and very active pieces.

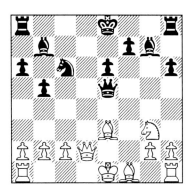

17 ♗d3 ♘b4

By winning the bishop pair Black's advantage takes a more concrete, material form.

17...♕xb2 is not in the spirit of the opening because after 18 0-0 Black's initiative is considerably undermined.

18 0-0 ♘xd3 19 ♕xd3 ♖d8

Polugaevsky instructively continues to pursue the initiative vigorously, ignoring White's queenside. Black is interested in bigger fish!

20 ♕e2 h5!

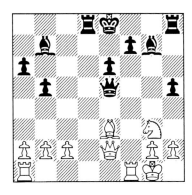

Black begins the next wave of his attack. It is important to take away the h5-square from White's knight. 20...0-0 21 ♘h5 gives White unnecessary counterplay.

21 ℤae1

A centralising move which achieves little. 21 ♕f2 is White's best chance, when 21...♕xe3 22 ♕xe3 ♗d4 23 ℤae1 ♗xe3+ 24 ℤxe3 gives Black the advantage in the endgame due to his superior minor piece, although there is still plenty of play left in such an endgame. 21...0-0!? is also possible, and dangerous for both sides.

21...h4 22 ♕f2

This now comes a move too late.

22...ℤd7 23 ♘e2 h3

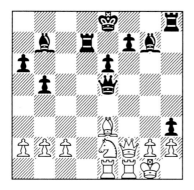

Ripping open the vulnerable light squares around Nezhmetdinov's king.

24 gxh3

24 ♗d4 invites the queen sacrifice 24...♕xd4 25 ♘xd4 ♗xd4 26 ℤe3 hxg2 27 ℤfe1 ℤh3, when Black is winning.

24...ℤxh3 25 ♘g3

White rushes to guard the sensitive h1-square but, unfortunately for him,

his king is simply too weak to withstand Black's onslaught.

25...♕d5 26 ♗b6 ♗e5

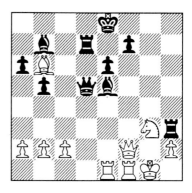

The threat of ...ℤxg3+ forces White to give up the exchange.

27 ℤxe5 ♕xe5 28 ℤe1 ♕g5 29 ♗e3 ♕g4 30 ℤf1 f5 31 ♗f4 ℤd1

It is well known that the side with the extra exchange should seek to exchange rooks in order to accentuate the advantage of the one remaining.

32 c3 ℤh4

The blockade of the f-pawn is successfully broken, forcing the gain of yet more material.

33 ♗c7

33 ℤxd1 fares no better in view of 33...♕xd1+ 34 ♘f1 ♕d5 35 ♘g3 ℤxf4.

33...f4 34 ♕xf4 ♕xf4 0-1

A fantastic attack, highlighting the potential power of Black's light-squared bishop in the Najdorf.

What would be your pearl of wisdom?

Well, I like this sentence very much – apart from the beginning, *God grant me*, because I'm an atheist:

God grant me the serenity to accept the things I cannot change,

The courage to change the things I can,

And the wisdom to distinguish the one from the other.

(Taken from The Prayer for Serenity, by Reinhold Niebuhr)

CHAPTER SIX

Sofia Polgar

Sofia (Zsofia) Polgar was born in Budapest, Hungary on November 2nd 1974, and is the middle child of the three Polgar sisters. The unorthodox background of the Polgar sisters has been widely reported. Their father Laszlo, a teacher, strongly believed that geniuses were not born, but created through the power of education, and therefore made it his mission to prove this theory. All three girls were educated at home and their day was divided into traditional education and up to ten hours of chess study.

The Polgars are the only family in the world that can boast three family members with the Grandmaster and International Master titles. Judit has a monster Elo of 2686, is presently rated the twentieth best player in the world, and is the strongest female player that the world has ever seen. Zsuzsa (Susan), at 2565 Elo, is the second highest female player, whilst Sophia is rated at fifteenth. Looking at these facts I believe that it can be safely assumed that Laszlo feels he has convincingly made his point. The cover of his book *Nevelj Zsenit* ('Bring up Genius') states 'I don't give a recipe, only a way of looking at things. I don't want to persuade anybody to bring up a genius, I just wanted to show that it was possible. I don't call upon or encourage anybody; people must decide what they want to do. I just hand over my pedagogical methods and lead people along the road I have already trodden, with the certainty that one can bring up a genius.' Many worried that the Polgars would become one-dimensional chess machines, but anyone who has spoken to them or followed their progress will know that they are intelligent, articulate, beautiful and 'normal' women.

Sofia's chess career began at what some would consider a very early stage. At the age of four she came third in the under-10 Budapest school's championship, and proceeded to win it the following year. 1986 saw the family travel to the world junior championships, where Judit and Sofia shared second place in the under-14 tournament behind Joel Lautier. The New York Open became a favoured tournament and one that they returned to for many years. Playing in the Big Apple in 1986 they caused a family sensation. Sofia was the co-winner of the Class-A section with 7/8, Judit won the unrated section with 7½/8 and Susan missed a Grandmaster norm by just half a point.

Sofia's biggest breakthrough came in Rome 1989, when she ploughed her way through a field of five Grandmasters to win the tournament with 8½/9, achieving an unprecedented tournament performance rating of 2930 Elo. 1989 also saw her gaining her International Master title and visiting England for a match billed as 'Young England versus Young Hungary'. The talents of Adams, Conquest and Norwood were enlisted, and here is Dave Norwood's version of the match: 'My first tactical ploy had been to buy each Polgar a bunch of flowers to soften them up. Like most of my tactics that day, it sadly backfired.' Having successfully emerged from the first day's play at 7½-4½, our boys prepared thoroughly for the next day's games by partying until the next morning. Dave 'The Rave' Norwood was then woken at 7.00 a.m. by a frustrated Judit phoning him from the hotel dining room, demanding that he join her for breakfast, as he had promised the previous day. Feeling a little under the weather, the boys faded away and the Polgars tied the match 9-9. 'Before we left, the girls came to find us and said they had a present for us. They looked like the nicest three girls you could ever hope to meet in Sunday School. They solemnly handed us the three *ChessBase* computer printouts of all our games that they had used to prepare against us. And each one was signed 'with love from all the Polgar sisters!"

Now 26, Sofia is married and has a young family. Her chess commitments have consequently changed and, for the past few years, she has taught and lectured chess over the Internet. However, the popularity of this beautiful and intelligent woman has not waned and she receives constant requests for appearances throughout the world.

How do you look back upon your formative chess years, and what do you remember most clearly about them?

I started playing chess at the age of four. Of course, in the beginning it was only a game, but with time it became a profession. The result I'm most proud of is clearly my victory in Rome 1989 *(A victory which became known as 'The Sac of Rome' and was the highest performance rating of any player up to that date)*. At the age of fourteen I won the tournament with 8½/9, ahead of several Grandmasters. It was a performance rating of over 2900 Elo. This result shocked not only the press, but also myself. And I remember saying to myself, how can I ever do anything better than this? I never came close to such a performance again...

The other events that were both very exciting and fun were the junior events and Olympiads that I played in. Together with my sisters, we won Olympic gold for Hungary twice and I also received several gold medals for my individual performances.

The Olympiads are full of both delight and pressure. The whole of the chess world is there. I used to love walking through those huge halls – it would take a long time – to see all the friends that I sometimes hadn't seen for years. It's also quite a social event, with its parties and all. Chess is not really a team sport and there are enormous pressures sometimes, even between the team members, but the most exciting part is when you play for a medal for your country. In the critical moments every move has a heavy weight. You play not only for yourself, but also for your team-mates and all the supporters sitting at home, searching for good news in the press.

Of course, it's a great achievement to play in the Olympiads, and to win a medal makes you especially proud! After my first Olympiad, in Thessalonika in 1988, we were national heroes in Hungary. The Olympiad was a few months after the Olympic Games in Soul, at which Hungary won twelve gold medals. We were celebrated as the team that won the thirteenth lucky medal for Hungary.

(At the 1988 Olympiad the Polgar sisters brought about the end of total Soviet domination of woman's chess and ushered in a new era of Hungarian control. The Hungarian Olympiad team consisted of Susan 19, Sophia 14 and Judit 12, whilst the youngest member of the Soviet team was the then woman's world champion, Maya Chiburdanidze, who at that time was 28)

Was there a great deal of rivalry and competitiveness between you and your sisters?
We had some competitiveness between us, but not really that much. I was always very happy for my sisters' success.

Did you consider yourself to be a woman in a man's world, or just another chess player? Your sister Susan famously said 'When a man loses against me, they always have a headache or things of that kind. I have never beaten a completely healthy man!' Have you come up against such prejudice?
From whatever angle you look at it, chess is still a male dominated world. Even to-day, at an average tournament, the percentage of women competitors is generally not more than 10%. However, this is still better than when my sister Susan started to compete. Now men have got used to losing to us, and they make fewer excuses!

(Now, I've heard some pretty pathetic excuses in my time, but this article that I found in the Melbourne Herald Sun (1st April 1998) stands out.)
'Robert Cowley claims he would have won a state championship if his opponent's breasts had not got in the way. Mr. Cowley, 50, claims he was unable to keep his eyes off Ngan Koshnitsky's cleavage. Part way through the six-round South Australian state contest he complained to the organisers about the 24-year-old reigning Australian women's champion's penchant for revealing clothes. The bare flesh – plus the fact that she played 'very well' – had cost him the title and prevented him from concentrating on the game, he claimed.'

Miss Koshnitsky hit back – in my opinion justifiably – by saying:

'It makes my angry that he didn't think I was good enough to win. I believe that most men can't accept losing a game against a woman.'

Personally, I wonder if Mr. Cowley blames his every loss on some outside factor, or if he just has a problem losing to women? My advice would be simple. Keep your eyes where they should be – on the board!

Can you remember a distinct moment of advancement in your chess career, or was your progress made in small steps?

My chess developed slowly and steadily, until it somehow stopped and I wasn't willing to put more effort into improving. Chess is a wonderful game, but for me it's not enough. I want to study and do other things.

But chess still clearly means a lot to you. You don't play as much as you used to – do you miss it?

Chess is part of my life and it has given me a great deal. I grew up with chess in my family. Travelling to tournaments gave me the chance to visit more than forty countries and meet some very special people, including my husband.

Over the last two years I have worked with chess on the Internet, writing articles and teaching online. Of course, I follow the tournaments that Judit plays in. So, chess is still a part of me, but I compete much less, almost not at all. Sometimes I miss it, but not so much that I would give up other things in order to play again.

You have recently married a Grandmaster. Do you play much chess at home?

I must say that being married is wonderful, and I believe being a family is a blessing! We have our first son Alon, he's eight months old now and simply makes life beautiful and worth a lot more. My husband Yona *(Israeli Grandmaster Yona Kosashvili, whom she married on February 7th 1999)* is a medical doctor, so he has very limited free time and we therefore play very little chess at home, especially since Alon was born. When we do play, sometimes it's fun and sometimes it does get tense.

What would you say are the differences between chess today and when you first started playing?

When I was playing in junior events we had just started to use computers, and the information wasn't as scary as it is today. Nowadays, things seem to somehow happen faster, both on and off the board.

Today there are many more Grandmasters under twenty years old, and if you want to become one of the best you need big results as a teenager. There are fewer 'traditional' tournaments today, with many more rapid and Internet chess tournaments.

Most players tend to concentrate on opening preparation. How much emphasis do you think should be placed on improving other areas, such as tactical intuition?

The stronger you are the more important opening preparation becomes. Once you've become a Grandmaster, you mainly study openings and prepare against the opponents that you will play, but for a club player or weaker, I wouldn't recommend wasting much time on openings at all. Tactics and positional understanding are the most important elements of the game.

So what study techniques would you recommend to aspiring players?

At any level, analysing your own games is essential for improving your technique. I would also recommend solving tactical problems to keep your mind sharp. Studying both endgames and positional games are also important methods of improvement.

Do you think that blitz is an important study tool?

My sisters and I used to play a lot of blitz games. It helps you to think fast and maybe it is the reason why we don't usually get in time trouble. On the other hand, it doesn't give you time to think deeply. Some trainers are very much against blitz because of this. You shouldn't overdo blitz chess, but most of all it's fun, so why not play?

Is chess a language, and is it your first language? I know that you can speak many different languages. Do you think that this ability has helped your chess?

I don't know if chess is a language, it probably is. I speak Hungarian, English, Hebrew, Russian and a little of German and Esperanto. I don't think that these languages influenced or aided my play, but I do hope that if I start studying computer programming, chess will be of help there.

Would you say that chess was mathematical or artistic, or a beautiful combination of the two?

I think that it's a combination of the two, plus it's also a sport. I personally like the artistic aspect of chess most. I would sometimes even make mistakes, just for the chance of a beautiful combination! Even as a kid, I was interested in the artistic nature of chess and I liked solving and composing chess problems. Talking about art, today I like to paint.

(A popular story was '...The discovery by Laszlo of Sofia, late at night, sitting in the lavatory, with a chessboard on her knees, busily composing. 'Why won't you leave the chess pieces alone?' asked Laszlo. 'Daddy, the chess pieces won't leave me alone', replied the little girl.' – The Polgar Sisters, *by Cathy Forbes.)*

What qualities do you think make a great chess player?

Most of all, to be a good chess player you have to be a fighter.

What do you consider to be your best game?

I'm not sure if it's the best, but the most important one of my career was the game against Chernin, from Rome 1989.

Sofia Polgar-Chernin
Rome Open 1989
Sicilian Defence

---

1 e4 c5 2 ♘f3 e6 3 d4 cxd4 4 ♘xd4 ♘c6 5 ♘c3 ♕c7

Clever move orders are a key part of modern Grandmaster practice. Here Black uses a Taimanov move order to reach a Sicilian Scheveningen, without allowing some of White's more dangerous options, such as the Keres attack.

6 ♗e2 ♘f6 7 0-0 ♗e7 8 ♗e3 0-0 9 f4 d6 10 ♔h1

A useful move in many Sicilian systems. The king steps out of the way of potential tactics on the a7-g1 diagonal and, if White is feeling really aggressive, she can later consider a pawn launch on the kingside with ♖g1 and g2-g4.

10...a6

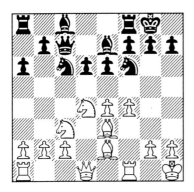

11 ♕e1

Another useful move. White prepares to switch her queen to the kingside and frees the d1-square for a rook.

11...♘a5

Black, for his part, seeks to access one of the key squares – c4 – which is relevant in so many Sicilian positions. 11...♘xd4 is the more solid option, exchanging pieces to reduce White's attacking potential. Then 12 ♗xd4 b5 leads to a typically complex position, with chances for both sides.

12 ♕g3

Perhaps White is too eager here. 12 ♖d1 looks sensible, intending to meet 12...♘c4 with 13 ♗c1, when White's pieces work in harmony.

12...♘c4 13 ♗c1

Now the a1-rook is closed out of the game.

13...b5 14 a3 ♕b6

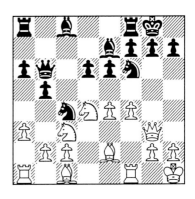

Black is striving to take the initiative from his lower rated opponent, but this move denies Black's knight an important retreat square – from b6 the knight can monitor the d5-square.

15 ♖d1 ♗b7 16 b3

Forcing the knight back.

16...♘a5 17 ♗f3 ♖ac8 18 ♗b2 ♖fd8?

Black, who has been directing making much of the play thus far, loses his sense of danger. White's queen, both knights and dark-squared bishop are ready to play a decisive role.

18...g6 protects Black against White's main threat. Then 19 ♘d5 exd5 20 ♘f5 ♗d8! defends for Black, when White can force a draw with 21 ♕g5 ♖xc2 22 ♗xf6 ♗xf6 23 ♕xf6 gxf5 24 ♕g5+.

19 ♘d5!

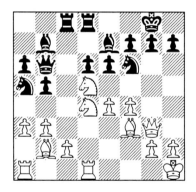

A typical Sicilian sacrifice, and a powerful one. Black must accept (or lose material), but there is no good way to take the beast.

19...♘xd5

Best of the available (poor) choices. 19...exd5 20 ♘f5 ♗f8 21 ♘xg7! ♗xg7 22 ♗xf6 is out if the question and 19...♗xd5 20 exd5 leaves Black with no decent options in view of the threat to the e6-pawn and the prospect of White's knight coming to f5.

20 ♘xe6!

White's knights show little regard for their own safety in the quest to attack the enemy king. There is only one way to deal with the mate threat.

20...g6 21 ♘xd8 ♕xd8 22 exd5

Polgar's alert tactical vision has won her a decisive material advantage.

22...♖xc2 23 ♖ab1 ♗h4

Black tries to generate counterplay but his pieces lack the co-ordination for this to be successful.

24 ♕h3 ♗c8 25 ♗g4

White is happy to exchange pieces as simplification is the clearest way to victory.

25...♗xg4 26 ♕xg4 ♘xb3 27 g3

27 f5 first is even stronger.

27...♗e7 28 f5

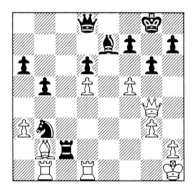

28...a5?

Missing his last chance in a difficult position. 28...♕c8 keeps the struggle going, although White is clearly in the driving seat after 29 ♕e4 ♕xf5 30 ♕xf5 gxf5 31 ♖e1 ♔f8 32 ♗c1!.

29 fxg6

Black lacks a way to recapture.

29...hxg6 30 ♕h3! ♖xb2

Black has little choice but to relinquish more material. 30...f6 31 ♕h6

♛e8 32 ♕e3! also wins for White due to the twin threats of ♗xf6 and ♕xb3.

31 ♖xb2 a4 32 ♖f2

White has her choice of ways to win but, true to the style in which she has played the game, she goes for the most direct route.

32...♘c5 33 ♖df1 f5 34 g4!

The opening of lines for the rooks on the kingside leaves Black with no hope of salvation.

34...♘e4 35 ♖g2 ♗f6 1-0

And what do you think is the best game ever played?

Adams-Torre, New Orleans 1920, is my favourite game

> ## Adams-Torre
> New Orleans 1920
> *Philidor Defence*

1 e4 e5 2 ♘f3 d6 3 d4 exd4 4 ♕xd4

This recapture was popularised by Paul Morphy, after whom the variation is named. Although the queen appears rather vulnerable on d4, tactical factors make it quite safe here.

4...♘c6

The obvious move, but perhaps not the strongest. 4...♘f6, with the intention of castling before attacking White's queen, may be Black's most prudent course.

5 ♗b5

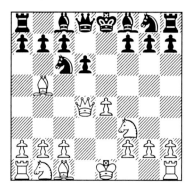

This pin helps White justify the early development of the queen.

5...♗d7 6 ♗xc6 ♗xc6

Black has acquired the bishop pair, but the commanding position of the queen and the extra space in the centre provide White with sufficient compensation.

7 ♘c3 ♘f6 8 0-0

8 ♗g5 is the modern aggressive main line in this variation, intending queenside castling and rapid centralisation.

8...♗e7

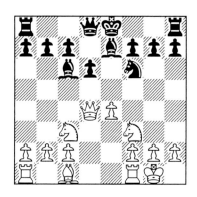

9 ♘d5

White opts for a policy of immediate central occupation.

9...♗xd5 10 exd5 0-0 11 ♗g5 c6

Black's position is somewhat cramped, prompting the fight for space on the queenside.

12 c4 cxd5

12...♘xd5 13 cxd5 ♗xg5 14 ♘xg5 ♕xg5 15 dxc6 bxc6 16 ♕xd6 gives White an edge thanks to his superior pawn structure.

13 cxd5 ♖e8 14 ♖fe1 a5?!

A difficult move to justify. Black wants to activate his queen's rook, but 14...h6, offering the king much needed breathing space, is far more useful, as we shall see.

15 ♖e2 ♖c8?

15...h6 is mandatory.

16 ♖ae1 ♕d7 17 ♗xf6 ♗xf6

17...gxf6, despite being horrible structurally, is the last chance to prolong the game.

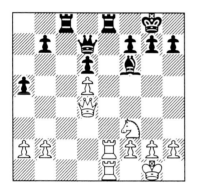

18 ♕g4!

The queens begin their dance of death.

18...♕b5

18...♕xg4 loses to 19 ♖xe8+.

19 ♕c4!!

Black's queen and the c8-rook are both needed to defend e8, so the queen must move once again.

19...♕d7 20 ♕c7!!

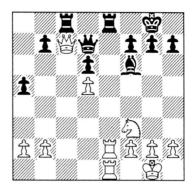

Black is given no respite.

20...♕b5

20...♕a4 21 b3 ♕b5 22 a4 is equally futile for Black.

21 a4!

Bizarrely there is a way for White to lose here: 21 ♕xb7? ♕xe2 22 ♖xe2 ♖c1 and this time it is White who is mated!

21...♕xa4 22 ♖e4 ♕b5 23 ♕xb7! 1-0

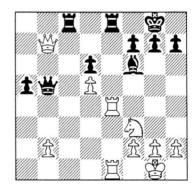

Black's queen has run out of squares from where e8 can be protected. A fabulous long-term combination, based on the weaknesses of Black's back rank.

What would be your peal of wisdom for the chess playing world?

Play for fun, not for ratings!

CHAPTER SEVEN

Julian Hodgson

London's own Julian Hodgson is an extremely well-known figure on the global chess scene. He is notorious for his explosive attacking style and consequently adored by spectators, yet he is feared by those who have to face him across the board. Commonly associated with Julian are the words 'chaos' and 'fireworks' and the nickname 'Grandmaster of Disaster'.

Since becoming a professional chess player he has made Open tournaments his speciality, winning major competitions across the world. The American National, Dutch and Canadian Opens and Cappelle la Grande (with an impressive performance rating of 2800) are just a few victories of one of England's premier Grandmasters. Julian is also a regular winner of England's extraordinarily tough chess Grand Prix, storming through in 1999 with a perfect 200/200, only the third time that this feat has been achieved.

Julian's name features on the British Championship trophy four times, the most notable being in 1992, when he cruised to victory with a record breaking, unbeaten score of 10/11. With Olympic gold and silver medals to his name, Julian has certainly put his mark on the chess world. He now teaches chess and cards in several London schools, and treats chess more as a hobby than a profession. However, he remains true to form, and if you are lucky enough to play Julian, sit back and wait for the fireworks.

Tell me about your chess playing background? How and when did you start?
I started when I was seven; my father taught me. I was into other games like patience and draughts and it seemed a natural progression to move onto chess. I think I picked up how it all worked within a day, it didn't take long at all. I started junior tournaments at eight, playing in things like the London Under-12s. I often played in older age groups, so obviously, if you're up against twelve-year-olds and you're only

eight, you're not necessarily going to win, but I did okay, I remember doing well.

At that stage, when you were entering tough junior events, was progress more important than victory?

I'm not sure. I think that I quite enjoyed both, I was always into winning. You've got to remember that there wasn't so much chess around then, certainly at junior level. It wasn't like it is now. You'd play in whatever was going on at the time.

Are you a chess player, or just a player? And why was chess your favoured choice?

I'm more of a player than a chess player, I just like playing games. But chess is the richest. It's very rich. There are lots of different ways to play and you know you're not going to get tired of it. I mean, a game like backgammon is relatively quite simple and it doesn't have the variety that there is in chess. Obviously there is a lot to backgammon but I think that chess is so rich and varied. It's just an excellent game.

Of course I should also mention something that probably everyone about my age and generation would say. Fischer-Spassky in 1972 really caught our imagination. I was born in 1963, so I was about eight or nine. The match went on at the height of the Cold War and it was a major hook, this American star taking on the Russian. It sort of hooked me into chess.

Did you have a coach as a junior?

No, they weren't really around then, it was a relatively new concept. I can remember Ray Keene coming to my house, but we would do more Latin than chess. He would help me with my Latin homework. There wasn't really much chess coaching for juniors then. There weren't that many good English players around.

Why did you become a professional chess player?

Well, I suppose because I was quite good at something that I enjoyed doing and I could actually make money at it. And, of course, when I first started it was before the Iron Curtain had come down and there was a lot more money in chess. It was a lot easier, a lot more relaxed. In a way, it was sort of the easy option.

What do you think has been your greatest achievement to date?

Well, I suppose the British result in 1992, when I got the all-time record with 10/11. That goes in the records and stands out above everything else.

Tell me about your feelings when you win your home championship.

Well, it was always one of my ambitions and obviously winning the first one in 1991, just before I was getting married, was a very nice feeling. I'd come close a few times, I'd been second the year before and I was very determined to win it and I played very well. It's something that I've aimed for, one of the main things that I wanted to do.

Then I did it again with a record score in 1992, and then, of course, 1999. I hadn't played in the British for a long time and I wanted to remind people that I could still play chess and that just because I'd become a teacher, this didn't mean that I couldn't play chess any more. I suppose that in 2000 I wanted to prove that 1999 wasn't a fluke. Normally, after I've won it one year, I want to come back and successfully defend my title.

Your executive chair at the British Championship in 2000 made headlines all around the world. What was the story behind it?

We were playing at a school and the thought of sitting on those little fold-up chairs – which are more suited to eight or nine-year-olds – for two weeks, well, I didn't think that my back would stand it. It wasn't really what I was looking for. I thought that in the interest of my general health and well-being, I should go and find a nice comfortable chair and then I wouldn't have any problems playing a nice long six or seven hour game.

And what was the fate of the famous chair?

It was actually won by someone in a competition that *(his good friend)* Dave Norwood ran in the *Daily Telegraph*.

You must have been extremely motivated to come back from a half point in the first two games. How did you motivate yourself and was Lizette a key factor?

Lizette *(Julian's wife)* is always a key factor, she's my motivation. Her attitude is that there's no reason to participate if I'm not going to give it my best shot. Especially at the British, of course, because there are no conditions *(Unlike many international tournaments, at the British Championships competitors must pay for their own accommodation costs and they receive no fees for playing)*. The only point of me being there is to win the tournament and go home with the £10,000 first prize. If I'm not going to give it everything I've got, then I might as well not play.

As to half out of two, it wasn't actually so bad. I lost to John Speelman and I always lose to Speelman, I've got a very bad record against him. It was quite nice to do it in round two. That way he couldn't bite me in round ten, when it would have been a lot more painful. So in a way losing that game made me a lot more free, I could play more like I used to play. I could go for it and be a lot more relaxed.

I was also getting so many jokes about the chair that I was very motivated to prove that it had nothing to do with the chair. I wanted to prove that it was the right thing to do. I thought that the only way to stop all the gags and not get teased for the rest of eternity was to win the tournament. So, I let my result speak for itself. There were a lot of things motivating me. Obviously, Lizette was a major force, but also justifying my poor chair, that was also a major factor.

(I again call upon the expert witness John Henderson of The Scotsman *for his view of the event)*

'When Hodgson brought his own executive chair a la Bobby Fischer to the tournament and began with 0½/2, he was, if you'll pardon the pun, the butt, of many jokes. However, laughing it all off, Hodgson rolled up his sleeves, made sure that the castors on the chair were well oiled, as he made up for his bad start with seven wins and two draws in the next nine rounds, to take the title for the fourth time with his lowest score.'

(As well as beginning with ½/2, fairly early on in the competition Julian also fell foul of the swarm of wasps that had made the tournament hall their home. Anyone who was unfortunate enough to be playing on board six, just off the demonstration boards, tended to be attacked by this rather vicious, chess hating collection of stinging, buzzing, evilness. On several occasions, play had to be abandoned when the sheer numbers made swatting ineffective. Clocks were hastily stopped as players leapt from their seats and fled. A particularly acrobatic wasp managed to land on the inside of Julian's spectacles, making for a rather tense and unforgettable moment as he carefully, but with tremendous speed, abandoned his glasses on the table. Players bought cans of wasp spray by the dozen, but when your author pointed out that maybe the organisers should empty the enormous bins, containing the remnants of vast quantities of food and fizzy drink more frequently than once a week, the problem was more or less solved!)

Where did the Grandmaster of Disaster title come from?

I'm not really sure. I think that it came from one of the journalists. It didn't really have anything to do with me. I think it was the idea that when I play I create disaster for my opponents. That's what I perceive it to mean, but in all honesty I don't really know where it comes from.

I found an Internet chess page entitled Captains of Chaos, which names you as their British hero because you give the impression of trying to create art on the board. Do you have an eye for chess beauty, and what do you think of Jon Levitt's assertion that 'A sophisticated aesthetic sense and appreciation of chess beauty go hand in hand with top class play'?

Maybe they wrote that a few years ago because I don't think I'm always like that today. Basically, when I'm playing people that I perceive won't be comfortable with chaos, I try to create chaos. I'm a great believer in playing to my opponent's weaknesses. If I believe that they are not happy with confusion on the board, then that is what I'll try and create.

Beauty is always in the eye of the beholder. I think that everyone has their own idea of what is beautiful in chess. I would say that I can see moves and games that I do consider to be beautiful, I do think that they are works of art, but everyone is their own judge. Everyone who plays chess has his or her own idea of a beautiful game. I think that maybe what Jon is saying is that you have to be a certain strength to appreciate some moves. You think, what a wonderful move that was – it doesn't look like anything fantastic or brilliant, but the idea behind it is very deep and very long-term and that was really quite a rich, beautiful idea.

What three words best describe you as a chess player?

Attacking, original and creative. These are the three words that come to me and they're probably how other people see me.

Why did you decide to make the Trompovsky your pet system?

With White the point is that you have greater freedom as to what you can do because you have that extra move. The beauty of the Tromp is that right from the second move you have the opportunity to get very rich positions, many different types of positions. I think that's the main attraction, as well as the fact that your chances of actually getting the opening are quite high, of course. And perhaps not being the hardest working player in the world, I do find it (unless you're looking at chess lines all the time) quite difficult to remember variations that are twenty moves deep, but I can normally remember to get my second move in! I still forget stuff in the Tromp, but I suppose the point is that people aren't playing against it all the time. You look at lines in the King's Indian and they have a lot of experience in that, but you look at the Trompovsky and they have to play stuff where they're not quite sure what is going on. I also don't know what's going on, so we're on a level playing field.

Tell me about being a chess teacher?

I think that the main thing I do is to try to encourage the children to get their pieces out and attack, because as you get older you tend to get more solid and positional. I'm a great believer in starting off with attack, using all your pieces and going for the king, going for checkmate. That's the fun bit. Basically, my thing is that chess is a game, it should be enjoyed. It doesn't have to be hard work. Once it becomes a grind and no fun, there is no point in doing it. I would say that playing attacking chess and having fun is the key.

But what is the key for chess success? Is it hard work? Should every chess player's motto be work, work and more work?

I think so. If you want to get good you have to work, especially in this climate. The way chess is going now, it's made for the person who is prepared to work very hard and, if you do, then you will be rewarded. To make it in chess these days you have to be very talented, that's just taken as read, it's not even an issue. And to make it to the top, you also have to be a phenomenally hard worker. Succeeding in chess is one of the toughest things out there, the competition is very fierce. That's why work, work, work is the key for people who want to get right to the top.

What about working at the board? Should you take an occasional break? And what goes through your mind when you leave the board?

Working at the board is, of course, absolutely crucial. You have to work hard at the board and the more you work, the better you will tend to play. On the other hand, I think that it's important to take the odd break during a game. Maybe get up, go for a little stroll, stretch the legs, maybe get a tea or some fresh air. At that point, normally I'm not thinking about the game. I'm wondering how Chelsea *(Football Club)* have done, or if England have lost another Test Match in the cricket. But I suppose if I'm really at my best, if I'm really playing well, then when I get up I'm thinking about the position. I would say that most of the time I'm not, maybe I'm not fully concentrated, but on those rare occasions I am, then I do tend to think about the chess position and I'm calculating variations in my mind. It depends on my mood really, and how energetic and hard working I'm feeling.

How important are tournament conditions and what difference do they make to your play?

As you get older, having good playing conditions gets more important. When I was younger I didn't really care much. But now my eyesight is not as good, and I do need good light, it's very important. If the light's bad, then I know I'm in for a lot more struggle. What a lot of people don't understand is that when you get to a certain level, when you get to be one of the top players in the world, you see much deeper into a position and to have that depth, you really need good conditions. You need the lighting; you need it to be quiet. You have to get into a frame of mind where you are incredibly concentrated. The better the conditions, the easier it is to do that. The strong Grandmasters go to levels that most people don't ever reach. If you're trying to see twenty moves deep into a position, then you really do need good conditions to get there.

In general the American tournaments have the best conditions. You'll play in the same hotel that you are staying in, so there's very little travel time. And they're nice big hotels with great lighting and air-conditioning, which means that it's not too hot and you can also normally get food whenever you want. The conditions are in general very good over there. These days, as I'm playing chess more as a hobby, more for fun, I like to play in good conditions. I want to enjoy it, which is difficult when the conditions aren't any good.

What chess story immediately springs to mind?

It has to be when I was Adams' second in his match in New York, his match in the Trump Tower against Tiviakov in the quarter-final stage of the 1994 world championship. Mickey had just won the first game with Black, it was a tough game. This meant he would have White in the second game. After I'd gone to bed, I woke up excitedly with a start at about three o'clock in the morning, because I'd found this very interesting variation where White sacrifices a piece for a big attack. I very excitedly told my wife, Lizette, who of course was thoroughly uninterested because she was so totally asleep. I also knew that I couldn't tell Mickey for a long time, because he likes to sleep until quite near the game – he does like his sleep.

So I only got a chance to tell him about this idea a couple of hours before the game. Normally, I don't think that he would have played it because we hadn't really had a chance to analyse it properly. But he got to the board, spent ten minutes thinking and decided that he'd better do this because Lizette had lost sleep over it...

So... don't keep us in suspense, what happened?
He won. He won a really nice game, took a 2-0 lead and went on to win the match.

You won the 1999 Grand Prix with an incredible 200/200. An intensely difficult achievement, but this is actually just a rather tenuous link to my next question. Eddie Irvine said 'Formula One is an exciting form of chess. There are so many routes of attack and scenarios are ever changing. It is an intelligent sport, so it never gets boring.' What would your response be?
I think that Eddie's got it in a nutshell. I agree with everything that he said. Maybe I should have become a racing driver and he should have tried his hand at chess. He's got it sorted. Chess in a nutshell!

Your enthusiasm and personal warmth seem to inspire other chess players. In 1999 eight-year-old Noah Belcher, who was selected for the All-America Chess Team, listed his career goals as becoming a Grandmaster, piloting helicopters in Hawaii and eating pancakes with you. Why do you think that you have this effect on people?
It's probably because people find my chess quite enjoyable. I've done the videos and they come across as fun and deep down I suppose I see chess as a fun game and something that people should enjoy doing. That probably comes through. That's what children want to do, have fun, win games and enjoy themselves. I think that I convey that attitude to a certain extent.

I'd be very happy to join him in Hawaii for pancakes some time.

Do you think that being a genuinely nice guy can work against you, or is your chess personality completely removed from your own personality?
I think that your personality comes out in your chess, they go quite well together. When you play you have to think that this is a business, you have to be professional and you just have to switch off. Obviously, it's difficult if you're playing people that you know and like. That's the side of it that I do find difficult to a certain extent. You just have to almost switch off from it. You must try and focus in on the game and try to forget whom you are playing. The only way to get around it is to concentrate on the actual chess itself.

Who is your favourite chess player?

Well, the four great players of my time are Tal, Fischer, Karpov and Kasparov. They all play wonderful chess, games which in their own way are works of art, masterpieces. I think that because the way I play chess is quite varied I don't have just one favourite player. I can really enjoy all the top players. When they've played a good game it's just a joy to play through.

Now a question from someone whom you may recognise! Your father wanted to ask 'When are you going to do some serious work?'

Maybe never, maybe sometime. I don't have a crystal ball. I don't know is the honest answer. I've sort of worked in the past and I probably will again. But when I look at the likes of Korchnoi, I think that the beauty of chess is that you don't ever really get too old to improve. As long as you have an open mind and are prepared to learn, you can still improve. And that's why, I may be thirty-eight now, but I can still see myself learning and improving at fifty.

What do you consider to be the best game that you have played thus far?

My game against Boris Gulko that I played in Groningen. I had a terrible score at this tournament, one out of nine or something, and I just thought 'Well, it doesn't really matter anymore.' I was White and I played with real freedom, a really nice game, a flowing game. Poor Boris looked stunned at the end of it. He didn't really know what had hit him. He couldn't complain because he'd lost a really good game. It's funny, because it's one of my worst ever tournament results, but my memory of the tournament is now that one game and I've forgotten about everything else. All I remember is this lovely game that I played against Boris.

(Julian was going through a terrible patch of poor form when he played the following game. In Attack with Julian Hodgson, Book 1 *he writes 'I had just lost my last two games in the 1994 Moscow Olympiad and then had begun Groningen with the fantastic score of 1 out of 8!')*

Hodgson-Gulko
Groningen 1994/5
English Opening

---

1 c4 c5 2 g3 g6 3 ♗g2 ♗g7 4 ♘c3 ♘c6 5 a3

The main line begins 6 ♘f3, but Julian has never been a fan of following theory.

5...e6

This invites White to try an interest-ing pawn sacrifice, although preventing the advance of the b-pawn requires a concession, e.g. 5...a5!?, surrendering the b5-square.

6 b4

6 ♖b1 is the solid move but, true to his style, Julian tries the most aggressive approach.

6...♘xb4

The best way to accept the sacrifice, and Julian admits that he missed it during the game!

6...cxb4 is the move he was expecting, when 7 axb4 ♘xb4 8 ♗a3 ♘c6 9 ♘b5 puts Black under pressure, while 8...♗xc3 9 dxc3 promises White good compensation thanks to Black's weaknesses on the dark squares.

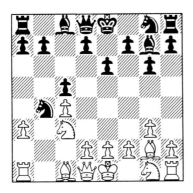

7 axb4 cxb4 8 ♘b5?!

Julian again chooses the most ambitious path, probably demoralised by his recent form and reasoning that 1/9 wouldn't be much worse than 1/8. However, in view of the note to Black's 9th move, discretion is the better part of valour.

8 d4 is more circumspect, when White can expect reasonable Benko-style compensation for the sacrificed pawn after 8...bxc3 9 e3 ♘e7 10 ♘e2 0-0 11 ♘xc3 ♕c7 12 ♕b3, as in Masculo–D.Gurevich, New York 1991.

8...♗xa1 9 ♕a4 ♗e5?

Black slips and suddenly White is back in the game, highlighting the fact that in sharp positions the assessment can often turn with one move. 9...♗f6! is the way for Black to refute White's exuberant play, as 10 d4 a6 11 ♘d6+ ♔f8 12 ♘f3 ♗e7 13 ♕xb4 a5 gave Black a clear advantage in Lobron–Kavalek, Bochum 1981, as Black's king will find sanctuary on g7, giving White no way to justify his material investment.

10 ♘f3 ♗b8

Boris has succeeded in keeping Julian's knight out of d6, but the price he pays is far too high. The bishop is effectively shut out of the game on b8, and its absence from the a1–h8 diagonal allows White to accelerate development.

11 ♗b2 f6

Practically forced as 11...♘f6 12 ♕a1 is very awkward for Black.

12 h4

Hodgson is in his element in unbalanced positions where he enjoys the initiative. In such a situation his creative mind can conjure up all sorts of nasty surprises to unsettle his opponent. The advance of the h-pawn is the quickest way for the h1-rook to join in the attack.

12...a5?!

It is very difficult to play accurately when defending such positions. There are few resources that even a strong Grandmaster such as Gulko can call on, other than the usual sensible approach of exchanging pieces and calculating variations as accurately as possible. With the text Gulko tries to hold onto his material gains but ignores the plan that Hodgson began with his previous move. Black will pay a heavy price for allowing White's rook free entry into the game.

12...h5 halts White's kingside assault and leads to a murky position after 13 ♕xb4 ♘h6.

13 h5 gxh5

13...g5 14 ♘xg5 (heading for e4) is not what Black is looking for, while 14 h6 is also awkward for Black.

14 ♖xh5

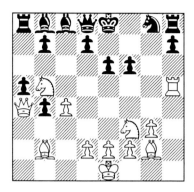

The rook arrives with great effect, making it hard for Boris to develop his kingside.

14...♕e7 15 ♘g5

The knight heads for the key e4-square, where it will target Black's weakened dark squares.

15...♖a6

Black also develops his rook in a way that is far from routine, but his motives are purely defensive.

16 ♘e4 e5

Black desperately tries to shut the troublesome dark-squared bishop out of the game, but Julian has more than one way to break down this pawn barrier, and the light-squared weaknesses that remain are irreparable.

17 c5!

White cements his grip on the d6-square and simultaneously makes queenside development more problematic for Black.

17...♔f8 18 ♘bd6 ♗xd6

Understandably removing the intolerable knight.

19 ♘xd6 ♖xd6

Returning material in order to break

Julian's bind. 19...♕d8 does not help because it invites 20 d4, when 20...exd4 21 ♗xd4 leaves Black struggling to find a move.

20 cxd6 ♕xd6

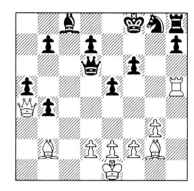

21 d4!

The dark-squared bishop has no opposite number and therefore Julian's main priority is to damage the pawns that obstruct this potentially powerful piece.

21...exd4 22 ♖d5 ♕c7 23 ♖xa5

The d4-pawn isn't going anywhere so White continues his policy of dismantling the dark-squared pawns. His opponent is no position to oppose this and must simply develop his scattered forces as best he can.

23...♘e7 24 ♕xb4 d6 25 ♖b5 ♔g7?!

Even the most desperate looking positions often contain resources of some kind, and here Julian is the first to point out that 25...♘c6 gives Black some hope of saving the game. After 26 ♗xc6 ♕xc6 27 ♕xd4 ♕xb5 28 ♕xf6+ ♔e8 29 ♕xh8+ ♔d7 30 ♕xh7+ White is certainly in control, but the bishops of opposite colour offer Black drawing chances.

26 ♕xd4

Now Julian's pieces dominate the entire board for the price of just one pawn.

26...♖f8

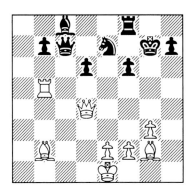

27 g4

The final assault begins. The strategy of releasing the b2-bishop is near completion, as White prepares to destroy the final obstacle on the a1–h8 diagonal.

27...♕d7 28 ♖h5

The rook returns to the square on which it entered the game with such great effect, preparing to attack Black's king.

28...♔g8

There is no escape in trying to exchange queens because 28...♕xg4 loses a piece to 29 ♕xg4+ ♗xg4 30 ♖g5+.

29 g5 ♕g4 30 gxf6 1-0

Black is powerless on the dark squares, his plight being illustrated in the following variations: 30...♕xg2 31 fxe7 ♖e8 32 ♕h8+ ♔f7 33 ♖xh7+ with total devastation, or 30...♕xd4 31 ♗xd4 ♘c6 32 ♗d5+ ♔h8 33 ♗xc6 bxc6 34 f7 mate. A fantastic attacking effort, particularly when one considers the psychological strain Julian must have been under at the time.

What is the best game ever played?

That's a monster question. One game that is not so well known was a game played between Joel Lautier and Peter Leko. Joel, he's the irresistible force when he plays these great attacking and intense games, and Peter is the immovable object. Joel basically started this attack in the opening and it continued until around the sixtieth move – a fifty move attack. It just went on and on and on. Peter Leko is this incredibly strong defensive player, but the attack was unrelenting. First Joel attacked the king on the kingside, then in the middle and then on the queenside. A ferocious onslaught that continued for so many moves. I actually told Joel that it must be one of the great games. It's not an obvious candidate, but just think about the huge amount of energy that this game would have taken out of them both.

```
            Lautier-Leko
             Ubeda 1997
           Sicilian Defence
```

1 e4 c5 2 ♘f3 d6 3 d4 cxd4 4 ♘xd4 ♘f6 5 ♘c3 e6 6 g3

6 g4 is the most aggressive move, launching the famous Keres attack. Lautier aims for a slower build-up, perhaps with the intention of luring Leko into a false sense of security.

6...♘c6 7 ♗g2 ♗d7 8 0-0 ♗e7

8...a6 is a typical move in Scheveningen systems, but Black is trying to do without it in order to save a tempo.

9 ♗e3

Both sides continue to mobilise their forces before commencing active operations.

9...0-0 10 ♕e2 ♕c7

Leko pushes on with his policy of doing without ...a7-a6. This provocative approach of encouraging ♘b5 has its pluses because it will be easy to evict the ambitious knight. On the other hand, Black loses the opportunity to make exchanges which would free his somewhat cramped position.

10...♘xd4 is the simplest way to try to equalise. Then 11 ♗xd4 ♗c6 12 ♖ad1 leads to a typically complex Sicilian position, with chances for both sides.

11 ♘db5!

The only way to take advantage of Black's omission of ...a7-a6.

11...♕b8 12 a4

A very important prophylactic move. Although Joel plans an attack on the kingside it is wise to restrain Black's natural counterplay on the other flank.

12...b6

Now 12...a6 plays into White's hands and meets with 13 ♘a3, heading for c4 with a clamp on the queenside.

13 f4 ♖d8

This seems reasonable but does not get to grips with the position. Black must begin active operations on the queenside with 13...a6 14 ♘a3 ♕c7, when White should continue his kingside attack with 15 g4 because 15 ♘c4?! is now met by 15...♖ab8, intending the liberating ...b6-b5.

14 g4!

Enough restraint! It's time to attack. The advance of the g-pawn will bring immediate gains as Black's knight will be driven to an inferior post. Meanwhile, White makes possible the rook swing ♖f3-h3.

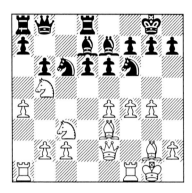

14...a6 15 ♘a3 ♗e8

Black must create an escape square for his knight.

16 g5 ♘d7 17 ♖f3

The h7-square is Leko's most vulnerable weakness so it is not surprising that Lautier now targets it.

17...♘c5 18 ♖h3 g6 19 ♖f1

With nearly all successful attacks it is important to bring up all available reinforcements before leaping into the fray, thus giving the attacker a far greater chance of achieving his objective.

19...♗d7 20 ♕g4

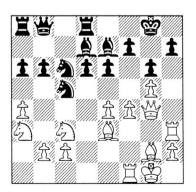

20...h5!

In the long-term the h7-pawn will prove very difficult to defend, so Leko takes the best practical decision and surrenders it under the most favourable circumstances in order to inhibit White's attack.

21 ♛h4!

Lautier shows he is up to the task and refuses to be swayed by the lure of material gain. 21 gxh6 allows Leko to shore up his defences with 21...♚h7, when it is hard to see how White can break down the kingside fortress.

21...♝f8 22 ♝f3

The point behind leaving Black's h-pawn untouched – for the moment – is revealed. It is an easy target for White's minor pieces and Joel chooses the direct approach. 22 ♞e2, bringing the knight over, also deserves consideration. From g3 the knight can pressure the h5-pawn as well as support f4-f5.

22...♝g7 23 ♝xh5 gxh5 24 ♛xh5 ♞e7!

With his kingside pawn shelter being ripped apart Leko needs to bring his pieces over to carry out the task that his pawns were doing.

25 f5

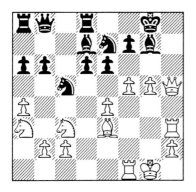

You have to admire Joel's approach. Nothing will stop him from getting to Black's king.

25...exf5 26 exf5 ♝xf5

The pawn must be prevented from reaching the f6-square at all costs. 26...♞xf5 27 ♞d5 is even stronger than the game.

27 ♞d5

Black's lack of control over the central light squares is fully exploited by this superb knight leap. He has no choice but to capture the beast before it wreaks devastation.

27...♞xd5 28 ♜xf5 ♛b7

The only way to defend f7 and d5.

29 g6

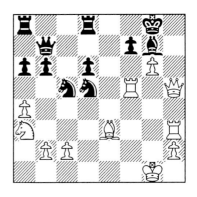

Again forcing Leko's hand with another double attack on f7 and d5. Black's king is under intense pressure.

29...♞f6 30 ♜xf6!

The tempo is relentless. Leko is not even given a moment to think about regrouping his defences because Lautier unleashes a blow with every move.

30...♝xf6 31 ♛h7+ ♚f8 32 ♝h6+

32 ♜f3? ♛e7! gives Black precious time to defend.

32...♚e8 33 ♛g8+ ♚d7

Forced.

34 ♕xf7+ ♔c6

34...♗e7 is well met by 35 ♖e3 ♖e8 36 ♗f8, exploiting the pin and threatening to queen the g-pawn. After 36...♘e4 37 ♕f5+ ♔c7 38 ♖xe4 ♗xf8 39 ♕f7+ White has a decisive advantage.

35 ♕xf6

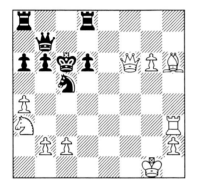

White has regained the sacrificed material but, more importantly, has excellent winning chances due to the powerful passed g-pawn and the exposed nature of Black's king.

35...♕d7 36 ♕f3+ d5

Allowing Lautier's knight to enter the fray, but Black's choice is severely limited. 36...♔c7 is well parried by the thrust 37 a5 b5 38 b4 ♘e6 39 c4, when Black's king will remain hopelessly exposed for the rest of the game. Note that 37...bxa5 falls foul of 38 ♗d2, threatening both ♖h7 and ♗xa5+.

37 ♘c4 ♕e6 38 ♗f4!

A star move which gets to the heart of the position. Although the g6-pawn is a thorn in Black's side the attack on the king takes precedence; not many players would have the courage to let their pride and glory go with check.

38...♕xg6+

38...♘d7 covers e5 but just makes

matters worse after 39 g7 ♕g6+ 40 ♔h1 ♕xg7 41 ♖h6+ ♘f6 42 ♕c3, when Black can already resign.

39 ♖g3 ♕e6?!

With both players struggling to reach the time control it is understandable that Black misses perhaps his best chance to defend, with 39...♕h7, when after 40 ♘e5+ ♔b7 White has no clear way in, although he still has sufficient compensation in view of Black's exposed king.

40 ♘e5+

With one move to reach the time control it is not surprising that Joel misses a clear chance to put the issue beyond doubt. After 40 ♖g7!, cutting off the king's escape route, Black must succumb to the onslaught, one possible continuation being 40...♘d7 (40...♖d7 41 ♘e5+) 41 ♘a5+! bxa5 42 ♕c3+ ♘c5 43 ♖c7+ ♔b6 44 ♕xc5 mate.

40...♔b7 41 ♖g7+ ♘d7

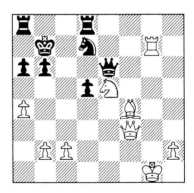

42 ♖e7!

Having reached the time control, Joel has plenty of time in which to find the win.

42...♕d6

The irritating rook must be left alone: 42...♕xe7 43 ♕xd5+ ♔b8 44 ♘c6+

♔b7 45 ♘a5+ ♔c8 46 ♕b7 mate.

43 ♗g3!

A nice retreat, paving the way for the queen to enter the game via f7. Such quiet moves in the heat of battle are often the most difficult to find.

43...♔c8

The king steps out of the pin but into further trouble!

44 ♘f7!

White's initiative has been sustained for twenty long moves and, with the text, Lautier makes it clear that there will be no escape from the relentless aggression.

44...♕c5+

Taking the knight costs Black his queen after 44...♕xe7 45 ♘d6+ ♔c7 46 ♘f5+ ♕e5 47 ♕c3+, while 45...♕xd6 46 ♗xd6 gives Black no hope of survival as both White's queen and bishop are ideally posted to hound the king.

45 ♔h1 ♔b7 46 ♘d6+ ♔a7 47 c4!

The d5-pawn is paralysed due to the prospect of mate on b7.

47...a5

The only way to get his king out of the firing line, but at the same time handing the enemy knight a fabulous outpost on b5.

48 ♕xd5

Lautier again uses good judgement. It would be tempting to keep the queens on the board in order to try and exploit Black's king position. However, he sees that he can maintain the attack in the endgame, too.

48...♕xd5+ 49 cxd5 ♔a6 50 ♘b5

The point. Black will have to return

the exchange due to his poor king position and lack of co-ordination. Leko is known to be a fan of Fischerrandom chess. Perhaps after this game he would prefer a game without kings!

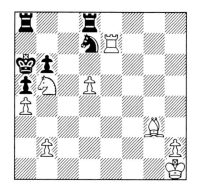

50...♘c5

No better is 50...♖ac8 51 ♗c7.

51 ♘c7+ ♔b7 52 ♘e6+ ♔a6 53 ♘c7+

Cruelly repeating moves.

53...♔b7 54 ♘xa8+ ♔xa8 55 d6 ♘xa4 56 h4

There is no need to defend the queenside because White's pawns will prove impossible to stop on the other flank and the bishop can take care of Black's efforts to promote.

56...♘xb2 57 h5

57 ♖c7 a4 58 d7.

57...a4 58 h6 a3 59 ♗e5 ♘c4 60 ♗f6 1-0

The h-pawn will cost Black a rook. A fantastic attacking game from Lautier, who maintained the momentum for many moves against an opponent who is highly renowned for defensive resourcefulness.

What would be your pearl of chess wisdom?

Play for the love of the game!

CHAPTER EIGHT

Emil Sutovsky

Emil Sutovsky was born on 19th September 1977 in Baku, the capital of Azerbaijan made famous by its first chess genius, Garry Kasparov. As you can imagine, having the world champion as your local hero was extremely inspirational. In 1991 Sutovsky and his family moved to Israel, where his chess career blossomed. 1996 was an awesome year for him. He stormed to victory in the World Under-20 Championships and was also awarded the Grandmaster title at the Yerevan Olympiad. In June 2001 he achieved a monumental victory in the European Championship, qualifying for the World Championship in the process.

He is currently ranked 25-27th in the world, his rating having leapt to a massive 2664 on the October 2001 rating list. As if this weren't enough, Emil is also a talented opera singer and has performed in numerous concerts around the world.

Can you tell me a little about your chess playing background?
I can't really say that I am a Soviet player now living in the West, of course not. But it was there in the Soviet Union that I got my chess fundamentals. For three years or so I studied at the Polugaevsky Chess School, which held sessions twice a year for two weeks. It had a great impact for many reasons, the pure chess reason and also the contact with the great masters who were also at the school. I also competed in a lot of the Soviet Youth Championships and jointly won the under-12 title with Sergei Movsesian.

A lot of the players that I know now, the top players, people like Peter Svidler and Alexander Morozevich, I've known since we were kids. We all competed in the *(Soviet)* Junior Championship of 1991, the last one before I left for Israel. I can easily remember twelve or thirteen players from then who are now in the top one hundred.

I had some really good trainers in the Soviet Union from the beginning of my career. In fact my first trainer was Oleg Privorotsky, who was also Garry Kasparov's first trainer! A few years later I started working with Valery Tsaturian but, if you remember, I lived in Baku, where the situation became quite sharp and Valery (who is still a very good friend of mine and gives me good and important advice from time to time) had to move away in 1988. So, at this stage I had two years without a serious trainer. I mean, I was training by myself, but at that time I didn't have a computer and it was really difficult to improve.

But I became a real chess player once I had moved to Israel. My rating was around 2245 when I emigrated here. Maybe I was already stronger, but there weren't enough tournaments that I could play in, so I wasn't a player, I was a talented junior. In Israel, I was given the opportunity to improve my chess and I started studying with good trainers and playing good players and my results improved rather rapidly. Soon after I had emigrated my rating was something like 2440. Then I started taking things more and more seriously. For two years I worked with Grandmaster Lev Psakhis and for the last four years I have worked with Grandmaster Alon Greenfeld, who is not just a trainer but a very good friend of mine. Having a trainer as a Grandmaster is not like when you are a kid and they show you all the variations, but when you have a lot of complicated stuff to do it helps to work with such a good player, to analyse the position, to find original ideas.

Why do you love chess?

It's a good question. Actually, I've never previously tried to formalise it. Why do you love somebody? I don't know, you just fall in love. You feel it like you need it. Ahhh *(as if hitting on an answer)*, I think it's because chess is such a great mix of many interesting things. Of course it's a game, but then it's something else as well. You have to apply your logical thinking. You can think of it like a game and then you can think of it like a science and when you play something that is really beautiful, you can enjoy it like you enjoy a piano piece.

In chess you have the motif of self-expression; you feel that you can win something with your fight, with your will, with your drive. I don't think that you get this in any other sport. There are great sports like soccer and basketball, they're dynamic and beautiful and people love them, but they don't have such a dynamic mix. When you play blitz chess, for example, it's pure sport. It's sport, it's adrenaline, you play and it's just a game. But if you play classical chess it's different; you come ready to predict, to foresee what your opponent will play. Once you are dedicated to chess you can use the feelings that you get, your intuition can help you a lot in everyday life. In fact, maybe this can apply to anything that you have to think over quite a lot and work on but, in chess, somehow you feel it. I think that it's one of the great factors.

Where do you see yourself five years from now?

Actually, I've never tried to guess this. Until now I have dedicated myself mostly to the chess calendar. I personally think that if you play chess as I do you should really work on it and have the ambition to aim for the very top. I think that you have to decide for yourself, do you have ambition, motivation, do you feel that you can do it? Then you have to try to be the very best.

I can't imagine setting myself a goal to be 2685 or something like this, of course not. Some players decide to retire despite achieving a very high level, even very good players like Matthew Sadler, for example (and Kamsky's example is the most drastic one, but here one may only guess the reason...). Matthew was a very bright player and very high rated, but he retired after a certain time. Some people have the possibility of just saying that they'll be a 2600 player. For some, this is possible, but at some point you'll have to combine your playing with becoming a chess trainer or something, which is not bad but just a bit different.

Looking at myself, I am a playing type of chess player. So I just think that I'll try to get as high as I can manage, which I can't predict, because part of the pure aspect of chess is good fortune and good invitations. Of course when you compete with the very top you become stronger and stronger, so I think that I'll dedicate myself to chess and hope to reach the highest standard.

What has been your best tournament to date?

There is no doubt that Ohrid was my best sporting achievement to date *(in June 2001, Emil won the 2nd European Championship in Ohrid, Macedonia)*. If we talk about tournament performance rating, the TPR, I've had a better result and scored something like 2820 Elo. But winning something like the European Championship is my main achievement. If you take into account also winning the tie-break, it is quite a deal, because after playing thirteen rounds I still had the power to play more chess. It was a really hard task, but I managed to do it.

In reference to your tie-break success, how do you remain calm when you have to win the last round or such a tie-break?

Remaining calm or cool is not an easy task, but it's not a big deal if you play at a high level. In the last round sometimes you make it, sometimes you don't, but being able to win last rounds is one quality of a good chess player. If you take someone like Gazza, when he has to do it, then he does it. We can recall many good examples, like Seville 1987 – last game of the match versus Karpov. Linares 1997 *(a category 17 tournament with an average rating of 2700 which included some of the best players in the world – among them Kramnik, Adams, Topalov, Polgar and Anand – where, instead of simply halving out in the final round, Kasparov dug his heels in and won a spectacular game against Vladimir Kramnik)* or the most recent Astana 2001 – once again, the decisive game against Kramnik. I think that it is an important quality for a player to know how to play in the decisive minute, but the tiebreak is a bit different. For example, my tie-break against Ponomariov, there was a great deal of pressure and a great deal of inspiration, but the chess itself suffered a lot.

So let's talk about the European Championship itself?

The tournament was a really tough one, but very interesting because it was the strongest ever open tournament. There were approximately one hundred and forty-four Grandmasters there *(144 Grandmasters and 38 International Masters – in total 204 competitors from 39 countries fighting for 46 FIDE World Championship qualification places).* In an open tournament like the PCA 1993, the average rating was stronger, but there were only fifty players *(The Professional Chess Association was formed in 1993, when Kasparov and Short broke away from FIDE in order to run their own World Championship cycle. The tournament to which Emil is referring was a World Championship qualifier held in Groningen that the majority of the world's leading players attended).* Here we had a really huge number of top players and good Grandmasters, forty players over 2600. So, a result like this means something.

For me this result is my best by far. I think that my play at the tournament was quite good, except maybe at the beginning, because I couldn't get used to the new time control. There is a big difference between this time control and playing classical chess. Of course you can't erase the good stuff just by a new time control and I did manage to play a few good games, but at the beginning you experience a lot of trouble, especially on the second time-control, which is only fifteen minutes. It forces you to make quite a lot of mistakes. As far as I understand the time-control that we are playing now is kind of an intermediate one; I don't think they *(FIDE)* will stick with it.

Good or not is another question. For classical chess it's a bad idea to shorten the time-control, but from another side, if they manage to get TV, media attention or new sponsors then it is worth a try. We can work with chess and try to create something new, but I think that this difference is only interesting to the chess players themselves and the chess lovers. I doubt that it will achieve much, but if it does, then it was a good decision and a good idea at the beginning. Now it is hard to say objectively whether it is good or bad, but I think that we can still play good chess under this time-control.

(FIDE announced their new time controls on 26th December 2000 (do these people not believe in Christmas or should we be slightly more cynical about the inconvenient timing of this declaration?). The reduced time limit of 40 moves in 75 minutes, then 15 minutes for the remainder of the game with an increment of 30 seconds per move from move one, caused controversy across the world. At the Gausdal Troll Masters 2001 a petition was started and signed by every one of the 48 competitors. It stated that:

'Undemocratic methods going against the statutes and ideals of FIDE have been used, without warning to immediately impose an intolerant decision, which might seriously hurt the future of chess, above the heads of both the world's chess players and their chess federations. We would like to express our concern for the idea of shortening time limits for all international title tournaments.'

Author of the petition: international arbiter Hans Olav Lahlum.

In the face of such widespread protest those at FIDE appeared to retreat from their original position and allowed an interim period in which the time-control was not mandatory, but they implied that soon this would be the case:

'I can see that some Federations are not yet prepared to accept the inevitable changes that our sport must undergo, if it is to move with other sports of the modern era' – Kirsan Ilyumzhinov.

FIDE claim that the main purpose of shorter time-controls is to increase the popularity of chess, to attract media attention and sponsorship. But, for example, I put it to you that reducing a game from six to four hours will not make it instant television material. Imagine a four hour boxing match, the boxers circling each other warily, only throwing punches every twenty minutes. This is not what the general public expect of their entertainment. As Jonathan Rowson wisely put it: 'It takes some patience to appreciate chess, and this is not as fashionable a virtue as it used to be!'

Chess does not have time for the usual televisual pursuits of violence, singing and people making fools of themselves. Imagine four hours of chess with Grandmaster karaoke, fancy dress or pie throwing etc. No! (Although the image of Kasparov in a rabbit costume singing YMCA does have a certain appeal!)

Why should we demean our great sport in any way? I totally agree with Larry Parr's assertion that what sells chess is not shorter time controls but: 'What has sold theatre since the time of the ancient Greeks? Aristotle noted about 2400 years ago that people go to the theatre not to see the Chorus (say, the 100-man FIDE candidates tournament) but to see the tragic heroes. In our terms, it means that people want to see a shootout on Main Street at High Noon. If the gunfighters are enemies, or best friends accosted by cruel circumstance, then so much the better. That's drama, that sells.'

The matches that have grabbed the public's attention have been great battles such as Fischer-Spassky, all-American hero against the evil Soviet empire. Kasparov-Short, reigning, powerful world champion against the British underdog. And who will ever forget the insults that they exchanged? Nigel Short started his world championship campaign strategy with a scathing article published in The Sunday Telegraph *in which he publicly insulted Kasparov:* 'He paces up and down the tournament hall like a baboon. But I don't want to sink to the level of the animal to beat the animal.'

Maybe I'm being overly dramatic, but the previous system produced great games and great champions. So why change a system that works? Okay, rant over, now back to the interview...)

What was you reaction to the Ponomariov scandal in Ohrid?

(The story goes that Ponomariov pre-arranged an 11th round draw with Aseev but then changed his mind one hour before the game. Therefore Aseev came to the game unprepared and angry, and lost. This unsportsmanlike behaviour has sparked a wave of condemnation and many have called for Ponomariov to be stripped of his silver medal and banned from playing in international events. Fortunately, Aseev still qualified for the World Championships.)

I think that it's one of the greatest sins of a chess player. I was really surprised. We all know about pre-arranged draws. Okay, it's not legal, but it's a very minor sin.

Even if it's not officially legal, it's quite okay and a normal situation for the chess world. Of course, a lot of players do it. I don't tend to much, I can recall a couple of times in three or four years and just with my good friends, or my trainer.

But to refuse it just before the game! I know that Ponomariov went to him *(Aseev)* an hour before the game, but it still smells bad. They agreed a draw at about 10:00 a.m. and at about 2:00 p.m. Ponomariov came to him and said 'Well, I have to play this game.' It was like an hour before the game, I heard it from Aseev himself. Ponomariov used the excuse that he had to consult his sponsor or something, but he's a big guy and he has to accept responsibility. Maybe it can be explained by his inexperience, but he has been playing chess at a high level for five years and I don't think that this kind of explanation is enough. And I don't really understand why Ponomariov, who is an extremely talented chess player, who has a great deal of support (including financial) in the Ukraine, did this. People will remember this issue for a long time to come.

Your win in Ohrid ensured your qualification for the 2001 World Championships. What will be your preparation to ensure success in this event?
The world championship system is not exactly to my liking. I have experienced it twice and twice gone out in the first round. The problem is that you can't really prepare for this kind of event. Normally you don't really know the other players; you only get their names something like two weeks before. So I do not have any special preparations for the World Championships. I have my general preparation on my openings and middlegame, but as for special preparation, I do not have any planned.

I don't like to rate my chances before any tournament. It is much more important to go there and try to do my best and that's what I'm about to do.

Every chess player has weaknesses. How do you determine what they are and how to fix them?
I'd better not talk about that. I'd better try to fix them first and then I can tell you how I overcame them.

Fair enough, but Garry showed weakness at the BrainGames Championship. If he cannot manage to fix his weaknesses how can we expect to overcome ours?
There is no question that Garry played poor chess in London, but he is still the strongest player. This is not just my opinion; he's managed to prove it numerous times after London, for example Wijk aan Zee and Linares.

(Wijk aan Zee 2001 was the strongest ever Dutch tournament, a monster Category 19 competition, the average rating an unbelievable 2710. Having obviously recovered from his BrainGames shock Kasparov was again playing at his best, coming ahead of his nemesis Kramnik by a full point. Linares 2001 was another Kasparov rout, where he finished three full points ahead of the

following pack.)

Of course Kramnik was stronger and his win was well deserved, it's beyond any question. I do not know the problem that Kasparov suffered at this match, but it was not the Kasparov that we're used to seeing.

(During the London match, the undiscerning British press, desperate for some concrete reason to explain Kasparov's poor play, spread rumours about a custody battle with his ex-wife Maria. Kasparov vehemently denied these rumours after completion of the match. The truth was – as he himself admitted – that Kramnik had simply out-prepared him: 'The match went wrong from the very beginning, in the face of superior and admirable preparation and play by the winner of this match. I just ran out of energy because I had to work ten hours a day to change the entire course of my opening strategy. Probably most of the mistakes were made in preparation last summer.' Taken from a press release on completion of the BrainGames Championship.)

To lose in this way, not winning a single game in fifteen, it is totally untypical for Kasparov, who is known for his victories. It was surprising that he played this way but, knowing him, he's a highly ambitious chess player and I believe that he will desperately try to get the title back. I think that it's still possible. We're used to him being on the top and we think of him as being older, but he's only thirty-eight. I think that he still has a lot of power and energy and that if he plays another match with Kramnik he has very reasonable chances to get the title back. The problem is how it will work with Kramnik. I don't think that it will happen soon.

As to the general weaknesses of chess players, if you think about professional chess players at the top level, in most cases they know why they have lost the game. When you play at this level sometimes you can play too hard for the win, overstep some boundary and lose the game. This is the main reason for losing.

When you play someone like Kasparov, Kramnik or Anand with Black you can simply lose out of the opening. You can get a really bad position on move twenty. You can get a position with which you are unfamiliar, they will just continue to play strong moves and you are almost without any chance of saving the game. It can happen, and not only against the top players, but also against other strong players.

At Grandmaster level it's not common for tactics to be the reason that you lose, but it is much more so at a lower level. If as an example I take some recent games of mine, out of six losses four of them were because I tried too hard to win the game. Sometimes you have an advantage, but can't find anything more than a draw, but you risk it anyway and, at the end of the day, you may find that you have lost the game. That can happen of course. But this is one of the differences between different types of players.

If you look at Karpov, or even Kramnik, they used to lose a very low number of games. They tend to get an advantage but sometimes fail to win, so the game ends in a draw. There are also some players, to which group I belong, that try too hard and are punished for that, but we seem to win more games. So, our chess style is much more to the liking of the spectator. For example when I played in Ohrid, I managed to win eight games, all of them against Grandmasters, quite remarkable.

I'm proud that in Ohrid I declined ten draw proposals, which is unusually high, even for me.

Draw offers are one of the reasons that we are not yet in the Olympic Games. In no other sport can you agree a draw during the competition. You can't play forty minutes of football and then say, well, I'm a bit tired, let's go for a draw and prepare for the next match. It can only happen in chess.

The International Olympic Committee recognised chess as a sport in 1999. Do you feel that this recognition has made any differences to the world of chess?

As for now, I don't feel any differences or any impact from this decision. They were talking about introducing chess as an Olympic sport, but I've heard that you can only enter as an individual about eight to ten years from now. So, if we can't enter it like other Olympic sports, I don't think that we will profit from this decision. For example in Israel chess is not yet considered a sport, so the chess players don't receive support from an Olympic committee or something like that. I hope that things will change but, until now, I've not seen any benefit from this decision. I can only hope that it will happen one day.

So, what can we do to raise the profile of chess?

I don't know how to draw people into chess. I think FIDE is working in the right direction now. Of course there are a lot of critics of Ilyumzhinov, but I think he has already made a lot of things better. Not only helped the chess world but saved the chess world. I can't imagine the World Championship system working without him. He has good contacts, not only as the President of FIDE but also as a politician. If they had something in mind to get chess into the Olympics as a normal Olympic sport then okay, if one day that worked, then it would be fine. But what can we, the chess players, do about it? I just don't know. I think that the power and the decisions are in the hands of FIDE.

Is losing more painful than winning is pleasurable?

It differs. Sometimes it can be, of course. When you play a very good game and you have a fantastic position, you find a very strong middlegame idea and you play just brilliantly and then you make one mistake and you lose the game, of course it's painful. If yesterday you won against a player who was 2200, just by playing your preparation, knowing that the line was winning, well, you've still lost the other game, despite playing brilliantly and that will be much more painful.

But normally, if you win a game, if it's a well deserved win, if you feel you've played well, then probably it would be on the same level. There has been much discussion about this. Karpov and Botvinnik always said that it was better to make two draws than win and lose, because when you lose you really suffer from your loss, whereas if you make two draws then maybe you suffer twice but you suffer just a little bit. Tal always said that he would prefer to win one and lose one, because if he played for the win and it happened that he lost, then that's fate.

Personally, winning a bad game doesn't bring me any special pleasure, but if you ask other top players, they would probably think differently about it.

Weaker players have trouble correctly evaluating positions. Does this skill simply improve with time or can you specifically work on it?

It's a good question, actually, and one often asked by club players. Of course it's not easy to understand why one position is better and one position is worse if there is nothing particularly wrong, like a very bad pawn structure. I think that there are two aspects to this; one of them is your own practical play.

So, you've played more or less the same openings for quite a long time and you're facing quite a good opponent. You get a pawn structure – pawn structure is one of the key points of chess – and you have to decide what are its advantages and disadvantages. For example I played a game against Grandmaster Sakaev in the European Championship. At one point I could liquidate into the endgame but then he would play ...f7-f6 and break my centre. So I played h2-h4-h5, forcing him to answer with ...h7-h6. The difference is, well, a very very minor difference, that when his pawn is not on h7 but on h6, his only plan is still ...f7-f6, after which the g6-square would be weak. You get this type of chance when playing these positions and you understand what the small things are that can have a great impact on the outcome of the game.

The second aspect is studying classical examples. This was very common and very useful in the Soviet Union and Soviet chess schools, but is not used too often by western chess players (we're not talking about the top players, of course!). These days the young study, they know everything and then a little bit more about modern chess, but sometimes they miss out on knowledge from the old masters, from people like Rubinstein, from the guys who made our game of chess, who formed the basis of the knowledge which we use now.

So, in order to become a better player and to understand what makes a position good or bad, you have to play by yourself and try to analyse the reasons for your loss and also study the chess classics.

What is the most entertaining tournament that you have played in?

Actually, I tend to play entertaining games. If you pay attention to the way I play, I can hardly name a tournament where I didn't sacrifice something serious. One tournament that I played in Harplinge, Sweden in 1998 was very special. During the tournament I managed to sacrifice the whole set. Something like a queen to Julian Hodgson, a rook to one of the local players, another rook to the German Grandmaster Schmaltz. I mean it was the whole set. It was a really funny one. As you would expect with this kind of play I didn't make first place, but I didn't play badly either. I scored six out of nine and, for a category thirteen tournament, it wasn't bad. It really was a fun tournament. After, when I looked at the games, it was kind of inspirational. It was not always the best play, but from a creative point of view it was extremely positive play.

Does chess still provide us with infinite variety?

We still have a lot of interesting things in chess. The Fischerrandom system and all that other stuff, well, I think that until now it's been for pure entertainment and nothing to do with classical chess, and I do not see any problem with classical chess.

Fischerrandom Chess

Chess players, myself included, seem to be only vaguely aware of the existence of Fischerrandom without knowing what it really is. This is what I discovered about it:

The game is played on a normal chessboard, using regular chess pieces. These are the rules:

1) All the pieces move as normal.

2) The pawns start in their usual places.

3) The positions of White's pieces are randomly chosen by a computer, to satisfy the following conditions – the king must be placed somewhere between the two rooks and White must have one light- and one dark-squared bishop.

4) As per usual, Black's set-up must mirror that of White.

5) Castling is done under the normal rules and (for White) 0-0-0 means moving the king to c1 and the rook to d1, while with 0-0 the king moves to g1 and the rook to f1. Okay, you're thinking, I always castle like that, no big deal, but imagine how strange castling would be if this was your starting position:

Leko-Adams
Fischerrandom Match 2001

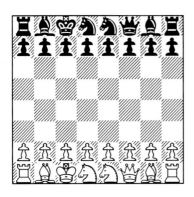

1 e4 e5 2 ♘d3 f5 3 exf5 e4 4 ♘e1 ♘d6 5 ♘e3 ♘xf5 6 f3 ♘xe3 7 ♗xe3 exf3 8 ♘xf3 ♗d5 9 c4 ♗xf3 10 ♕xf3 ♕xf3 11 gxf3 ♘e6 12 f4 c5 13 f5 ♘d4 14 ♗xd4 cxd4 15 ♗e4 ♗e5 16 ♔c2 ♔c7 17 ♔d3 ♖ae8 18 c5 ♗f6 19 b4 ♖e5 20 ♖he1 ♖he8 21 ♖e2 d5 22 cxd6+ ♔xd6 23 ♖ae1 ♖8e7 24 ♗g2 ♖xe2 25 ♖xe2 ♗e5 26 h3 ♖c7 27 ♖e1 b6 28 ♗e4 h6 29 a4 ♖c8 30 ♗b7 ♖b8 31 ♗e4 ♖c8 32 ♗b7 ♖b8 ½-½

Bobby launched his new chess variant at a press conference in Buenos Aires, 19th June 1996. Times have changed since he won the World Championship in 1972, and I can see how he would consider the sheer volume of opening theory available to be strangling the creativity of the game at which he excelled.

Random chess eliminates opening theory, as there are a possible 960 starting positions. It forces both players to rely on original strategy from move one and reintroduces the creativity that is some-times lost under mountains of theory. Fischer chess is aimed at demonstrating who is the stronger and more talented player, not simply who is better prepared, who can remember larger chunks of moves or who has the better computer or team analysis. In front of the assembled press Bobby also pointed out that the serious study necessary to play classical chess made it too much like hard work and that the reason he played chess was in order to avoid work!

Now that we're wiser, I'd like to hand you back to Emil...

Actually, the 'death of chess from draws, everybody knows everything' – this has already been announced twice, if I remember correctly. Once in Capablanca's time (Jose Raul Capablanca 1888-1942), when people thought that they knew everything and that the draw was forced: 'You play the Queen's Gambit and then it is just a draw'. And the second instance in Karpov's time. If you look at the tournament tables there were about 75% draws. But nowadays, in very, very tough tournaments, decisive games are around about the 50% mark.

Again, I don't see any problem with classical chess. If one player in every second game can still prove that he knows what to do better than his opponent, then I don't see what the problem is. There are still a lot of things to investigate in chess; there are still many gaps in our knowledge. If you take a look at old books, you can see that we have changed our minds about very basic positions. We said it should be like that, but then one day we found something new. So I think that for the next few hundred years we won't have a problem with running out of options. Even if computers become too strong, I still think that we'll play. There's still a lot of play and a lot of creativity left. Maybe, in ten years or so, we'll stop playing machines.

What do you think is your best game?

Until now I think that the best one was against Boris Gelfand in the 2000 Israeli Team Championships. First, the game was not decided by direct attack. Nor was it a purely positional game where he made one inaccuracy and had one weakness for the whole game and I just pushed and won.

It started with a very interesting opening idea and then over the board I managed to find a very unusual sacrifice which led to a very nice combination. Then he found a brilliant defence, playing three or four only moves to remain in the game. Then, after I got the advantage, he defended so very well that I had to find another two very powerful moves to improve my position further. But still he held on and the game took something like sixty moves. So, I had to overcome him in the open-ing, the middlegame and then in the endgame, which is quite a classical approach to beat a player. And, of course, Gelfand is the strongest player that I've beaten, which is going to have a certain impact.

(Emil was kind enough to provide annotations, and these are in Italics, marked ES.)

Sutovsky-Gelfand
Israeli Team Championship 2000
Sicilian Defence

1 e4 c5 2 ♘c3

ES: I had bad memories from our encounter in the 1999 League, when I opted for the main line in the Najdorf. This time, I decided to go for something else....

2...d6

Not the ideal move if you are going to face the Grand Prix Attack, but there is no choice if, like Gelfand, the Najdorf is your main defence to 1 e4. If Black plays a different move here White can head back for the main lines with 3 ♘ge2 and 4 d4.

3 f4 g6 4 ♘f3 ♗g7

Black deliberately leaves his queen's knight at home in order to make ♗b5 ideas less appealing.

5 ♗c4 ♘c6 6 0-0 e6 7 d3 ♘ge7 8 ♕e1

Part and parcel of any self-respecting Grand Prix player's armoury. The queen prepares to swing out to h4 in the event that Black should foolishly castle kingside.

8...h6

Of course, world-class grandmasters are never so obliging.

9 ♗b3 a6 10 a4

ES: I'd already played this position twice before the current game, against Psakhis and Gelfand. In both cases I preferred 10 ♗d2. Sutovsky–Psakhis, Israel 1999 continued 10...b5 11 f5!? (an interesting pawn sacrifice; 11 ♘h4 b4 12 ♘d1 was agreed drawn in Sutovsky–Gelfand, Tel Aviv 1999) 11...gxf5 (11...exf5 12 ♘h4) 12 ♘h4 f4 13 ♗xf4 ♘e5 14 ♕g3 ♖g8 15 ♔h1 ♕c7 16 ♘f3

♗h8 17 ♕h3 ♘g4 18 ♗xh6 ♗xc3 19 bxc3 c4 20 dxc4 bxc4 21 ♗a4+ ♗d7 22 ♗xd7+ ♕xd7 23 ♗g5 e5 24 ♕h7 f6 25 ♗c1 ♕e6 26 ♘h4 0-0-0 27 ♘f5 ♘xf5 28 ♕xf5 ♕xf5 29 exf5 ♖h8 30 h3 ♘h6 31 ♖b1 ♔c7 32 ♖b4 d5 33 ♗e3 and White was clearly better.

10 e5 was all the rage for a while, especially after Anand beat Gelfand convincingly with it in 1996. However, recently Black seems to have found the antidote with a plan based on ...♘f5 and ...d6-d5. Consequently Sutovsky goes for the more conservative approach.

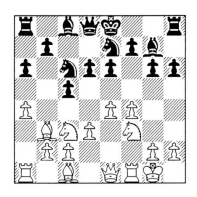

10...♖b8 11 ♗e3 b6

ES: Black covers the c5-pawn, but this move is not the best. Stronger is the natural 11...0-0 12 ♕h4 (12 ♕f2 b6! 13 d4 d5!; 12 f5?! gxf5 13 ♕h4 ♘g6 14 ♕xd8 ♖xd8 15 exf5 exf5) 12...♘d4 (12...f5 13 ♖ae1) 13 f5 ♘ec6! 14 f6 ♕xf6 15 ♕xf6 ♗xf6 16 ♗xh6 ♗g7 with equality.

It seems strange that, having prepared ...b7-b5, Black opts for a more passive option. However, there are tactical problems with the alternative – 11...b5 12 axb5 axb5 13 e5! highlights the weakness of Black's dark squares on the queenside and in the centre, for after 13...♘f5 14 exd6 ♘cd4 15 ♘e4

White has the initiative. *ES: 15...♗b7?! 16 d7+! ♕xd7 17 ♘xc5 is very good for White.*

12 ♕h4

Another prophylactic move, making the ...d6-d5 pawn break more difficult for Gelfand to achieve.

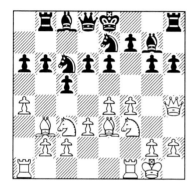

12...♘a5

12...d5 is inadvisable as White has 13 exd5 exd5 14 ♘xd5 (14 ♗xd5 is also possible) 14...g5 15 ♘xe7, the queens sacrifice enough for the advantage after 15...gxh4 16 ♘xc6 ♕c7 17 ♘xb8 ♕xb8 18 a5 etc. In this line 14...♘xd5 leaves Black a pawn in arrears in the endgame after 15 ♕xd8+ ♔xd8 16 ♗xd5 ♘b4 17 ♗b3, when the attempt to restore material parity with 17...♗xb2 allows 18 ♖ab1 ♗c3 19 ♗xf7 ♘xc2 20 ♗xc5 with a winning position.

13 ♗a2 ♘ec6

Sutovsky is widely feared as a dangerous attacking player, so this attempt to exchange queens is understandable but does have the drawback of removing a possible defender of the kingside.

14 ♕g3

ES: Now Black's knight on a5 is misplaced and White starts his attack.

14...♘b4 15 f5!

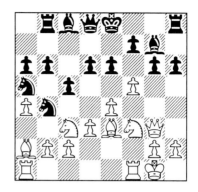

A very uncompromising move, typical of Sutovsky's style.

ES: It's the only way to exploit Black's weak king and under-development.

15...♘xa2

Rather than take his opponent on in a tactical slugfest Gelfand seeks to take the sting out of White's attack by exchanging the dangerous light-squared bishop. 15...♘xc2 is critical. Then 16 fxe6 ♘xe3 leaves Black a piece to the good but facing a strong attack, 17 exf7+ ♔d7 (17...♔f8? 18 ♘h4) 18 ♕xg6 leaving White with a strong pawn on f7 and Black with an exposed king. White's lasting compensation for the sacrificed piece is demonstrated in the following variations: 18...♗xc3 19 e5 ♔c7 (19...dxe5 20 ♘xe5+ ♗xe5 21 ♕e6+ ♔c7 22 ♕xe5+ ♔b7□ 23 ♕xe3) 20 bxc3 ♘xf1 21 ♖xf1 ♖f8 (21...dxe5 22 ♘xe5 ♖f8 23 ♕xh6) 22 e6 (these variations are based on those of Bangiev in *Chessbase Magazine*).

16 ♘xa2!

ES: 16 fxg6!? was very interesting and I saw that my attacking chances were quite high. Nevertheless, spending about 40 minutes over my 16th move, I discovered that 16 ♘xa2 promised more and I played the objectively

strongest move, in my opinion. 16 fxg6 ♘xc3
17 gxf7+ ♚xf7 18 bxc3 ♚g8 19 ♘h4
♘c6! 20 ♘g6 ♖b7! 21 ♖f2 (21 d4!?)
21...♘e5 22 ♘xh8 ♚xh8 23 ♖af1 ♚h7
24 d4 ♘g6! is unclear.

16...exf5 17 exf5 ♗xf5 18 ♘h4
♗e5

This intermezzo is forced due to the
threat, if the bishop retreats, of ♘g6,
e.g. 18...♗e6 19 ♘xg6! etc.

19 ♗f4! ♗xf4 20 ♕xf4 ♗e6

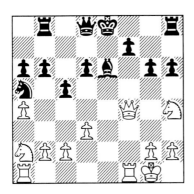

21 ♘xg6!!

Without this White's attack would be
in serious danger of running out of
steam. Now Sutovsky comes into his
element.

21...fxg6

21...♖g8 is just asking for trouble after 22 ♖ae1.

22 ♖ae1 ♕e7

ES: Gelfand finds the best defence!

22...♚d7? is disastrous as 23 ♖xe6!
smashes through.

23 ♘c3

White uses every piece to attack
Black's frail defences.

23...♚d7 24 ♘d5

Obliging Gelfand to sacrifice his
queen.

24...♗xd5

24...♕g5 is the only alternative but it
is easy to see why Gelfand rejected it
because 25 ♘f6+ ♚e7 26 ♖xe6+ leaves
Black defenceless after 26...♚xe6 27
♕e4+ ♕e5 28 ♕xg6.

25 ♖xe7+ ♚xe7

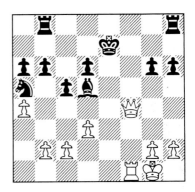

With two pieces and a rook for a
queen Black is doing fine in terms of
material, so it is White's duty to maintain the pressure before Black is allowed
to consolidate.

26 b4

It is understandable that White wants
to open a second front on the queenside in order to deny Black's king a safe
haven, but Sutovsky misses a golden
opportunity here in the shape of the
more accurate 26 ♖e1+ ♚d7 27 ♕g4+.
Black lacks a good square for his king,
e.g. 27...♚c6 (27...♚d8 28 ♕xg6) 28 c4
and White is well on top.

26...♘c6

Of course not 26...cxb4?! 27 ♕d4,
which fully justifies White's previous
move.

27 ♕f6+ ♚d7 28 c4

Forcing Black to jettison material if
he is to stay on the board.

28...♘xb4 29 cxd5 ♘xd5 30 ♕xg6

The exposed position of Black's king

takes priority over the (level) material situation, giving Sutovsky all the winning chances.

30...♖be8 31 h3

While Black's king is stranded, the white king lives in comparative safety.

31...♔c6 32 ♖f7 ♖hg8 33 ♖g7

ES: 33 ♕h7! is stronger, maintaining the threats against Black's king.

33...♖e1+ 34 ♔f2 ♖ge8

ES: 34...♖xg7! 35 ♕xg7 ♖e6, with the idea of pushing the b-pawn, gives Black counterplay. Then 36 ♕a7! is an interesting manoeuvre, aimed at paralysing Black's pieces and stopping the queenside pawns: 36...♘c7 37 g4! ♖e8 38 h4! and, suddenly, White's kingside pawn majority decides the fate of the game: 38...♖a8? 39 ♕xa8+ ♘xa8 40 g5 hxg5 41 h5 etc.

35 ♕xh6 ♖8e2+ 36 ♔g3 ♘e3

This counterattack would cause many players to panic, especially when it comes from a top grandmaster, but Sutovsky keeps a cool head to negotiate the threats.

37 ♕h7 ♖xg2+ 38 ♔f3 ♖xg7 39 ♕xg7

ES: Now the h-pawn is the decisive factor and the position is winning.

39...♘f5

39...♘d5, to give Black's king some extra support and prepare an advance of the queenside pawns, is the more prudent course. Then White is denied the possibility available to him in the game since 40 ♕a7 ♘c7 cages the queen!

40 ♕a7 a5 41 ♕a8+ ♔c7 42 ♕a7+ ♔c6 43 ♕b8

With Black denied his queenside counterplay the h-pawn should decide the issue in White's favour.

43...♘d4+ 44 ♔f2 ♖e2+ 45 ♔f1 ♖e3 46 h4 ♖xd3

He may have won a pawn but Gelfand has also allowed the h-pawn to accelerate towards its goal.

47 h5 ♖d1+ 48 ♔g2 ♖d2+ 49 ♔h3 ♖f2

ES: 49...♖d3+ 50 ♔g4 ♖d1 51 ♕a8+ ♔c7 52 h6.

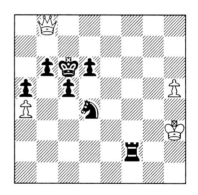

50 h6

Black will have to part with his rook in order to stop this pawn from fulfilling its destiny.

50...♖f6 51 ♕a8+

Setting up a skewer along the 7th rank.

51...♔c7 52 h7 ♖h6+ 53 ♔g2 ♖xh7 54 ♕a7+ ♔c6 55 ♕xh7

The rest is a simple matter of technique.

ES: The rest is quite simple. The curious thing was that a few weeks prior to this game I played an ending with queen against knight and three pawns and won it rather easily, against IM Barsov.

55...b5 56 ♕a7 b4 57 ♕xa5 ♔d5 58 ♕b6 b3 59 a5

White's a-pawn speeds matters up considerably.

59...♔c4 60 a6 ♘b5 61 ♕xb5+

♔xb5 **62 a7 b2 63 a8♕ ♔c4**

Gelfand must have been hoping for a miracle to continue playing in so hopeless a position.

64 ♕a2+ ♔c3 65 ♔f2 d5 66 ♕a3+ 1-0

A far from perfect game, but a good example of modern grandmaster chess – hard fought every step of the way, with White getting the better of the skirmishes.

And what, in your opinion, is the best game ever played?

It's so subjective that it can hardly be said, but I could pick Kasparov-Topalov *(already chosen by Yasser)*, maybe because it's so fresh in my mind and it was a really ingenious combination. It's really hard to say, but this was a really great game.

I can name a dozen of the great games which I like enormously. Probably Kasparov would be my favourite here, too, as I can recall Karpov-Kasparov, Game 16, 1985 *(also already chosen, this time by Johnny Rowson)* and Karpov-Kasparov, Game 22, 1986, and would include both as my most memorable games.

But of course, every World Champion and many top players have their ingenious creatures.... I have great respect for many players who didn't manage to become World Champion but whose names will never be forgotten – to name but a few: Rubinstein, Nimzowitsch, Bronstein, Keres, Geller, Korchnoi *(as for Victor Lvovich, (Korchnoi)* he is still capable – like a good wine he becomes better and better with the years!)

Kasparov-Karpov
World Championship 1986
Queen's Gambit Declined

1 d4 ♘f6 2 c4 e6 3 ♘f3 d5 4 ♘c3 ♗e7 5 ♗g5 h6 6 ♗xf6

In the Queen's Gambit Declined the freeing ...♘f6-e4 is often a good try to equalise, ensuring that at least one set of minor pieces is exchanged. By taking on f6 immediately White rules out this idea at the cost of relinquishing the bishop pair.

6...♗xf6 7 e3 0-0

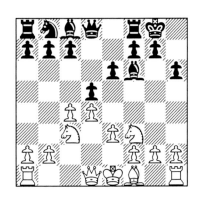

8 ♖c1

White is in no hurry to develop his light-squared bishop as one of Black's

---

main ideas is to capture on c4 and then break back in the centre with ...c7-c5. Thus if White can delay the development of his bishop until capturing on c4, so much the better.

8...c6

Black opts for the other central break, based on ...e6-e5. This move fortifies the centre in preparation for ...♘d7. 8...a6 is the other way to play the position, when White probably does best by continuing to wait for ...dxc4 with 9 ♕c2 or 9 ♕d2.

9 ♗d3

Now if Black goes for a plan based on the thrust of the c-pawn he will lose as much time as White, so it is time to develop the bishop. These finesses are certainly not amazing but, at this level, every small achievement must be fought for.

9...♘d7 10 0-0 dxc4 11 ♗xc4 e5

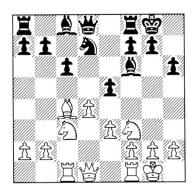

Black has more or less committed himself to this pawn break with his 8th move, and now wants White to open the position for his bishops with 12 dxe5.

12 h3

Instead Kasparov agrees to an IQP position.

12...exd4 13 exd4 ♘b6 14 ♗b3

Chances are approximately level from the opening stage. White has extra space but a structural disadvantage, while Black has the bishop pair but also the inability to properly blockade d5.

14...♗f5 15 ♖e1 a5 16 a3 ♖e8 17 ♖xe8+ ♕xe8 18 ♕d2

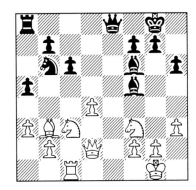

18...♘d7?!

This move, which weakens Black's control over both the central squares and the light squares on the queenside, is Karpov's first error. The knight also limits the mobility of Black's queen. 18...♕d7 is natural, and after 19 ♖e1 ♖e8 20 ♖xe8+ ♕xe8 21 ♕f4 ♗e6 22 ♗xe6 ♕xe6 23 ♕b8+ ♕c8 24 ♕a7 ♘c4 Black was comfortably holding his own in Portisch-Van der Sterren, Ter Apel 1994.

19 ♕f4 ♗g6

19...♗e6 20 ♖e1 is a little awkward for Black.

20 h4

White grabs some extra kingside space. The key to this position, from White's point of view, is to not do anything dramatic but to improve his position as much as possible, without allowing Black to break out from his slightly cramped quarters.

20...♕d8 21 ♘a4

Kasparov clamps down on the ...c6-c5 pawn break and eyes the c5-square as a potential outpost for his knight.

21...h5

Preventing any further kingside expansion but handing White the g5-square.

22 ♖e1 b5

With the rook vacating the c-file Karpov takes the opportunity to claim some space on the queenside and chase away the irritating knight.

23 ♘c3 ♕b8 24 ♕e3

A prophylactic move, preparing Black's next by defending along the third rank.

24...b4

Karpov cannot resist the temptation to simplify the position.

25 ♘e4 bxa3

25...♗xe4 doesn't work on account of 26 ♕xe4 bxa3 27 ♕xc6 axb2 28 ♕d5, winning material.

26 ♘xf6+ ♘xf6 27 bxa3 ♘d5 28 ♗xd5 cxd5

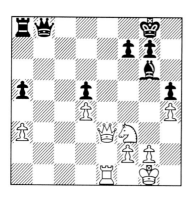

29 ♘e5

An instructive position. Most players are led to believe that bishops are slightly superior to knights in all but the most blocked of positions. Here we have a knight that definitely has the edge. Black's main problem is the d5-pawn, which restricts the bishop and could easily become a target.

29...♕d8 30 ♕f3

Targeting Black's most vulnerable points on h5 and d5.

30...♖a6 31 ♖c1 ♔h7

31...♖f6 32 ♕h3 ♗f5 33 ♕e3, followed by ♖c5, gives White a definite pull.

32 ♕h3

Leaping at the chance to organise a back rank invasion.

32...♖b6 33 ♖c8 ♕d6 34 ♕g3

Kasparov piles on the pressure. Karpov, meanwhile, is struggling to find anything constructive.

34...a4

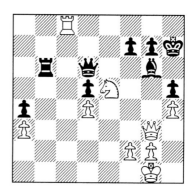

35 ♖a8

Hitting the a-pawn and setting a diabolical trap.

35...♕e6

Black has no convenient way to defend a4. 35...♖b3 looks tempting until you see 36 ♖h8+ ♔xh8 37 ♘xf7+, winning the queen.

36 ♖xa4

White reaps the first rewards of his hard work. The first pawn falls.

36...♕f5 37 ♖a7 ♖b1+ 38 ♔h2 ♖c1

Threatening ...♕b1, but this is easily parried.

39 ♖b7 ♖c2 40 f3 ♖d2

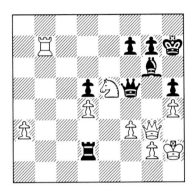

Karpov is making it as difficult as possible for Kasparov to utilise the extra pawn but he is hampered in his counterattacking efforts by his poor king position.

41 ♘d7

41 ♖b4 is plausible but Kasparov chooses to finish the game by direct attack.

41...♖xd4 42 ♘f8+ ♔h6

42...♔g8 43 ♖b8 is clearly hopeless for Black.

43 ♖b4

An excellent move. It is very impor-tant to put a stop to Black's attempts to solve most of his problems with ...♕f4.

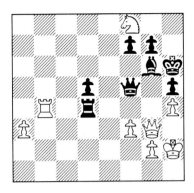

43...♖c4

What else? Karpov is seriously tied up and his king is in terrible danger. 43...♖xb4 might lead to the following amusing double queen endgame: 44 axb4 d4 45 b5 d3 46 b6 d2 47 b7 d1♕ 48 b8♕ and, despite having the move, Black's queens are unable to either attack or defend, e.g. 48...♕c1 49 ♘xg6 ♕xg6 50 ♕h8+ ♕h7 51 ♕gxg7 mate.

44 ♖xc4 dxc4 45 ♕d6

Black is tied up and has little option other than to run the c-pawn and hope for the best.

45...c3 46 ♕d4 1-0

The threat of ♕e3+ can only be met by the loss of the c3 pawn. With Black's king still stuck out on a limb there is no hope of survival.

What would be your pearl of wisdom for the chess-playing world?

What, like my chess motto? I would really like to find something both in my heart and in my head, as without this kind of approach I do not believe that one can get to the very top of chess.

We can remember your great compatriot Churchill who said, 'Whatever happens to us, we should fight, fight and fight until the victorious end.'

CHAPTER NINE

Jonathan Rowson

Jonathan was born in Aberdeen, Scotland on 18th April 1977. His junior chess career successes included representing Scotland throughout his schooling and silver medals at the European Under-18 Championship in 1995 and Under-20 in 1997. He made 1999 an extremely noteworthy year by graduating with first class honours from Oxford University and becoming Scotland's third and youngest Grandmaster. He also won the Scottish Championship (an achievement he repeated convincingly in 2001, beating the previous year's joint winners in consecutive rounds and sealing victory with a round to spare).

Christmas 2000 saw him plough his way through a pack of higher rated Grandmasters, including ex-British Champion Julian Hodgson, to take first place with an unbeaten score of 7/10 and a rating performance just short of 2700 in an event in York. The clearly unbiased reporter for The Scotsman, John Henderson, wrote: 'Once, on a tourist trip to the city of York, I discovered in the local museum that there's still in existence an ancient bylaw that legally allows you to shoot a Scotsman within the confines of the city centre with a bow and arrow on a Sunday afternoon. In reality, this may have been the only way the competitors might have stood a chance in stopping the run of Jonathan Rowson in the pre-Christmas York Vikings Chess Festival.' Jonathan has also written two popular chess books, *Understanding the Grünfeld* (1999) and *The Seven Deadly Chess Sins* (2001).

Could you tell me a little about your chess playing background?

My family enjoys a mild dispute over who taught me the moves. At the age of five, either my mum, Uncle Michael or late Grandad Rae started it all. Thereafter my brother used me as a chess punching bag until one day around the age of seven I exchanged all the pieces and, with just kings remaining, I shouted upstairs to my mum in wails of delight. She was doing a different sort of 'hoovering', so didn't hear me, but thereafter I started to punch back, and continued to develop my love of chess at school and at the Bon Accord Chess Club in Aberdeen.

I first represented Scotland at primary level, at the age of nine, but I made some sort of leap when my family moved to London when I was ten years old. There I met Richard James at the Richmond Junior Chess Club, who introduced me to the possibility of improving by studying books as well as playing.

When I returned to Aberdeen two years later my personal and family life were initially very complicated and I think I used chess as a very effective form of escapism. Every day I would return from school and study chess for at least an hour, usually more. Much of this time was spent daydreaming about co-operative opponents letting me win in style, but some of it was more serious, because I had an excellent first coach in the form of Scottish FM (FIDE Master) Donald Holmes, whom I used to see every few months. He encouraged me to play through game collections and practice analysis Kotov-style, by looking at a complicated position for a while, writing down conclusions and comparing them to the author's analysis. This is fine in theory, but it didn't happen as often as it should have, and even now I prefer to daydream. Anyway, I made considerable progress at this time and from being around 1600 Elo as a twelve year old, by the age of fifteen I was already somewhere between 2200-2300 Elo.

Who was your inspiration?

Inspiration comes in various forms, but it's no joke to say that I was my own inspiration. In the sense that making the most of myself, and living life fully really mattered to me.

For various reasons, including developing diabetes at the age of six, I became quite self-aware and self-disciplined at a young age and saw my life as some sort of project, perhaps even as a work of art, with myself as the artist. That may sound a bit grandiose, but I really thought of myself in that way; not that I was uniquely endowed with special talents or more worthy than others, but just that I realised that my life was my responsibility and that I was free to live it as well or badly as I would choose. Chess is rewarding in this regard because luck is more or less eliminated, so you begin to see a strong correlation between personal effort and better results.

There were people who helped a lot as I was growing up, including Paul Motwani, Mark Condie and John Glendinning. Then of course my mum, who has been a constant source of strength. I've always been somewhat bewitched by Kasparov's games, but I don't think I really had any chess heroes as such. Indeed my childhood heroes were more likely to be historical or political figures; Mahatma Gandhi, Martin Luther King junior and Nelson Mandela come to mind.

How important was becoming a Grandmaster, both personally and within the chess playing community, especially as your final norm was achieved in Scotland?

Very important. Inside the chess world, ratings probably matter more than titles in terms of recognition, partly because there are a burgeoning number of titled players in the world. I'm sure there are lots of Grandmasters who have never even heard of me, and many I don't know myself. So, there is a sense that the title has lost some of its allure, but it's still an honour to have the title, and it's by no means easy to attain.

By the time I was eighteen, it looked likely that I would eventually make the title if I continued to apply myself, but it was especially pleasing to do so in Scotland, all the more so since an English Grandmaster had been invited to make the norm possible, and I seized the chance while it was there *(The English Grandmaster was actually 'Aaron MacSummerscale' as he came to be known. We had a marvellous two weeks in beautiful Edinburgh and felt privileged to be a part of the creation of Scotland's third Grandmaster)*. On a personal level, I guess it's one of those things you can 'tell your grandchildren' but, nevertheless, it cannot sustain you for long. New desires quickly take hold.

What is your greatest ambition, and what is your plan to achieve it?

My deepest personal ambitions lie outside of chess, but certainly I would like to keep on working seriously on the game and improving steadily. It's important for me to feel that I made the most of my chess potential, but only within the context of my whole life. In this respect, I am aiming to be 2600 before I am thirty. This is a limited goal in one respect because 2600 barely makes the world top 100 these days, but it's also a difficult personal challenge, because there are other things going on in my life

However, this question reminds me of that saying: 'when all is said and done, more is said than done'. Indeed, when it comes to ambition it is crucial to distinguish between 'wanting' something and 'choosing it'. If, for example, you want to be World Champion and you tell yourself this every day: 'I want to be World Champion; that is my ambition' this feeling of 'wanting' will quickly become your experience and the experience will be one of lacking something in your life. If, on the other hand, you find that you can identify with yourself as being world champion, then you set about choosing it. You reveal your choice through your behaviour and your determination. Every action says 'this is who I am' and if your actions are dedicated to chess improvement, then you've made an appropriate choice.

Kasparov chose it from a very young age, as did most other champions. This is slightly more speculative, and I may soon be proven wrong, but I have the feeling that when it comes to beating Kasparov, Kramnik chose it whilst Anand merely wants it. As for me, to answer this question by stating my main ambition is just another way of saying 'I want this' so I prefer to pass for now.

Is there a history to your Gumptious ICC handle?

I was introduced to the concept of gumption when I read *Zen and the Art of Motorcycle Maintenance* by Robert Pirsig. This is one of my favourite books and I loved the conception of gumption as he expounds it. 'Gumption' appears to be an old Scots word from the 18th century, but its exact meaning is rather elusive. If you have gumption, or 'feel gumptious', then you have 'get up and go', you have a certain connection with the task at hand. Pirsig says that the gumption filling process occurs when one is quiet long enough to see and hear and feel the real universe, not just one's stale opinions about it.

I used this as my ICC handle because I am intending to write a book about gumption and wanted to remind myself of the relevance and importance of this project every time I found myself playing 'just one more' game of blitz like some sort of zombie. *(Jonathan is quite a regular on the Internet Chess Club, his highest Internet rating having so far been 3007)*

What is your most entertaining chess story?

The one about the madman, the assassin and the transsexual, but I prefer to keep the details for a less public forum.

Apologies for the abruptness of this question, but it was set by one of my readers and I feel obligated to ask it. Are you embarrassed to be a Grandmaster rather than something worthwhile like a brain-surgeon?

Embarrassed? Far from it. It is an important question, however, and such sentiments have troubled me from time to time. I guess the question implies that chess players are somehow 'useless' and one should be embarrassed unless your vocation has utility, especially if you have channelled your energies towards an activity which has little public value on the face of it, when you could have channelled yourself towards other areas. This claim can be undermined on all sorts of grounds, but it remains a probing challenge.

Firstly, being a grandmaster does not need to be a central part of your identity or even your vocation, so far from being an embarrassment, the title in itself is a great source of pride, recognising as it does a level of skill in a complex activity not commonly achieved by the majority of people.

Beyond that, Grandmaster Keith Arkell put it quite nicely when he said that although he felt he might not be doing much good for the world as a chess player, he was fairly sure he wasn't doing any harm. I'm sure there are lots of people in 'worthwhile' vocations that would find it more difficult to say this.

Moreover, the extent to which you are 'worthwhile' depends a lot on the company you keep, your morals, your motives and the value you bring to people around you. There are millions of unsung heroes in the world, millions of worthwhile family members whose value may be barely known outside the family, countless unpublished poets or little-known musicians whose work is certainly 'worthwhile' for them and those around them. Likewise, distinguished chess players may have a considerable influence on the chess community but, more importantly, this can also impact on the wider world in a variety of ways.

But I must admit, the question of chess being an essentially futile activity has a nagging persistence for me. Sir Walter Scott said chess was 'a sad waste of brains' and George Bernard Shaw said it was 'a foolish expedient for making idle people believe they are doing something very clever'. I occasionally think that the thousands of hours I've spent on chess, however much they have developed me personally, could have been better spent; I could have learned several languages in that time, campaigned for world peace or worked on cancer research. So on the face of it, the opportunity cost seems huge, but this is a limited perspective which does not capture the value of playing chess.

By way of justification, I think it was Hans Ree who poignantly remarked that 'chess is beautiful enough to waste your life for' and personally I often find chess extremely beautiful. However, this idea of 'waste' is perhaps what really needs to be attacked, because it assumes there is some sort of 'good life' which is not a waste. Theories abound, but no one really knows what constitutes such a 'good life'. Even if they did, it may have more to do with the quality of your thoughts and emotions than what you do to earn money.

Let me put it like this. There are some vocations that are essential to the preservation of human life (medicine), the smooth functioning of society (law and order, politics), the so-called 'creation' of wealth (business) and the development of skill and intellect (education). And there are others which are perhaps less essential from a functional perspective, but which play an invaluable part in human experience (art, leisure, sport, music, literature and, dare I say it, chess). Not everyone can be a brain surgeon, or wants to be, and let's be thankful for the fact that we have a variety of talents and experience to offer, thus enriching human life.

Lots could be said about this issue, which amounts to how we should live our lives, but in so far as there is an answer, it might be said that chess is a creative and beautiful pursuit, which allows us to experience a wide range of uniquely human characteristics. Grandmasters are capable of generating this experience to a level that is sometimes exciting and sometimes sublime and this is surely worthwhile, not only for themselves, but for anyone who can understand the game or appreciate the value of beauty. In any case, I would much rather live in a world where everyone had the freedom to choose how to fulfil themselves, and were relaxed about making mistakes, than a world where everyone was fiercely determined to be 'worthwhile'. A tree may be worthwhile for building a dam or making a fire, but it is no more so than a tree which is beautiful in virtue of the fact that it *is*.

Chess is a celebration of existential freedom in the sense that we are blessed with the opportunity to create ourselves through our actions and in choosing to play chess, we are celebrating freedom above utility. Besides, the grass is always greener on the other side and I'm sure there's a brain surgeon out there who curses the day he put the chessboard away and took out his scalpel.

Tell me about the seven deadly sins?

I'm hoping you mean the seven deadly chess sins because I haven't read the bible for a long time. The first thing to say is that I bring a slightly unusual conception of sin to the book, whereby sin is the state of fundamental limitation that we find ourselves in when it comes to chess. These limits are basic – our brains, nervous systems, emotions, habits, personality and desires. These are the raw ingredients of the chess struggle and they are all imperfect systems, leading inevitably to error. We are in a sinful condition in the sense that we cannot help but go wrong. My approach was to devise seven sins that were common to all players based on these limitations and then to elucidate them on the basis of the little I know about chess psychology and neuroscience. *(Jonathan describes chess sin as a misreading of chess reality. And goes on to say that if we are the main instruments of the chess reality, it is through a better understanding of ourselves that we come to understand sin in chess)*

THINKING is concerned with the way we perceive positions and go about working out what to play – I examine the role of emotion in this process and some of the problems and paradoxes which result when we realise that we perceive on the basis of pattern recognition.

BLINKING is basically about recognising critical moments in a game – we have no special tool or indicator to help us do this and our failure to do so is a fairly typical cause of error.

WANTING is about the way our desire for a win or a draw effects our play, and I also stress the importance of enthusiasm and being able to 'just play'.

MATERIALISM is based on an attack on our current point system in chess – pawn=1, rook=5 etc. We often fail to see good moves that give away material because this point system has become so hard-wired.

EGOISM is all about your own sense of self as you play, and how this relates to your awareness of your opponent.

PERFECTIONISM is about trying too hard and getting into time trouble.

LOOSENESS is about 'losing the plot' and the role of emotion more generally.

A recent study has shown that Grandmasters use a different part of their brain to amateurs, that Grandmasters rely on years' worth of stored information and pattern recognition. How do you view such research?

There have been very few studies on the chess brain from a neuro-scientific perspective and I suspect they would show that, on the contrary, we use the same part *(of the brain)* to a similar intensity, but that somehow (which we're probably a few years away from understanding) Grandmasters use it more efficiently and effectively.

De Groot and others constructed studies based on board reconstruction and chess 'vision', which showed that Grandmasters don't think more than weaker players, but they do 'see' more and what they see is more relevant to finding good moves. I have some problems with this idea because the 'vision' of strong players tends to be entirely abstract. Contrary to popular opinion, most Grandmasters don't actually have a chessboard in their head (not even a little one). It's difficult to examine your thoughts while thinking about something else, so I can't be too definitive, but all the top chess players I've asked tell me that they can talk about chess moves quite easily without any exact correspondence to a visual image of the board, so the 'vision' model may not be a full explanation. It seems that Grandmasters can somehow transcend the need for a visual image, and think about chess in some sort of mysterious realm of purely spatial relationships.

On an explanatory level, there are close affinities between excellence in chess and fluency in language. I think there are less than a hundred players in the world who really 'speak' chess as their 'first language' in this sense. Just as we don't usually make basic grammatical errors when we speak our native language, players who are deeply talented, who seem somehow to have chess 'in the blood' tend not to make basic oversights in the way that lesser mortals, even of Grandmaster strength, do. I haven't often played against such players, but Grischuk comes to mind, as do Morozevich and Adams in terms of having a seemingly effortless ability to home in on good moves almost instantly on seeing a position. So perhaps there is something like a 'factor X' at the very highest levels of chess, but that's just another way of saying that there are some things we can't explain yet.

Then, of course, you have strong players who have chess as a strong 'second language', including some Grandmasters and several thousand players of international standard. Then you have those who can 'get by' in the language but get easily confused and can't use too many words (see many positions) at the same time. Then you have those who struggle to speak the language, and make fairly major grammatical errors (blunder pieces) on a regular basis.

So, what about the theory from the same study that Grandmasters manage to programme themselves with 100,000 chess patterns?

It's misleading to say that Grandmasters programme themselves directly. It's not like the Grandmaster feeds himself with a certain number of patterns, which he later regurgitates (forgive the image). In my view it's the brain that makes the patterns on the basis of experience, so all the Grandmaster does is expose himself to chess information and lets the brain rack it up in its own mysterious way.

Moreover, we should not ignore the striking empirical fact that the vast majority of Grandmasters started playing when they were quite young and continued to do so intensely until they became Grandmasters. Thus they exposed themselves to chess when their brains still had a lot of 'plasticity' and the chess patterns could be near optimally organised. That said, all of our brain mechanisms are highly complicated and the question 'why did I play that move?' often remains unanswered, even for Grandmasters.

Following on from this, what do you recommend players like myself do to 'feed' themselves with patterns in order to better their game?

You certainly can improve significantly by working on your chess, but I'm afraid that although I like to believe in determined efforts at self-improvement, will power and free will, it may be that the margin for improvement is not especially wide. After stabilising at a certain level, your average player will tend to oscillate within a fairly narrow range.

Chess is probably more difficult than the most complex natural languages of the world, so for your average club player to become a Grandmaster is perhaps more difficult than an English speaker with no particular language skills learning to speak fluent Hungarian. I have some Hungarian friends and Hungarian is about as complex as languages get, but I know that even if I lived in Hungary and studied the language every day for ten years, I still wouldn't speak the language as well as they do now. Of course, I could make myself understood and, carefully avoiding mistakes, I might even sound proficient, but that's not the issue here. In pressure situations such as those we have in chess, fluency makes a big difference, and no matter how much I study, I'll never be close to Kasparov's fluency in chess.

I'm not a defeatist by nature, but there are definitely limits to what is possible when it comes to chess improvement, so I would say that the first step to improving is to set a challenging but realistic goal.

What are the secrets of the Grandmaster mind?

I'm not sure, and in any case they aren't really secret; or perhaps I'm just not in on the secret! Most strong players don't really know why they think of a certain move as good and another bad, partly because the mechanism for seeing the moves is based on spatial intelligence located in the right hemisphere of the brain and the mechanism for explaining these moves lies with language ability located largely in the left hemisphere. This is a bit over-simplified, but it points to the fact that the insight of a Grandmaster is often not easy to purvey. If I assess a position as clearly better for one side and my opponent thinks it's equal, I can't always explain my point of view verbally.

Certainly, Grandmaster 'secrets' are not a simple list of qualities like good preparation, physical fitness, precise technique, knowing the opponent, practicality, accurate and quick calculation, positional judgement etc. Although all these things are helpful, they are not fundamental. The bottom line is that most Grandmasters have a strong sense of where the pieces should go, but beyond the incomplete pattern recognition theory above, nobody is exactly sure why.

It has been said that chess is all about conquering the opening. Do you agree with this point of view?

In a word, no. Above strong Grandmaster level, say 2570, I think openings matter a lot and often have a decisive bearing on the game, but there are many super-Grandmasters who are not so good in the opening, who still make excellent results by outplaying their opponent later in the game.

Between 2300ish and 2550ish they are quite important and you can gain a lot of points through careful preparation, though the level of technique is not usually so high that you won't have another chance if you go wrong.

Between 2000 and 2300 it's rarely the most significant part of the game in terms of opportunities presented, but the outcome of the opening will often have a correlation with the final result.

Below 2000 it will only tend to matter in terms of specific preparation for specific opponents in fairly predictable sharp or trap-intensive lines. So, if you fall within this latter range, I would definitely spend more time studying interesting endgames, tactics and middlegames than I would on the opening.

That said, we're all a little indulgent in this regard because we can quickly see the result of opening preparation and identify with our openings in the way we can't with other, less labelled aspects of the game. So I genuinely believe that for most club players one hundred hours of endgame work will yield far more dividends in the long-term than one hundred hours on the opening, even if you see the benefits of the opening work more directly.

Beyond that, I genuinely believe that by far the best thing to do is to study your own games as deeply as you can and be as honest with yourself as possible. I also advise doing anything which will increase your enthusiasm for the game, even if that involves not playing for a while! Playing through well annotated games tends to be pleasurable and instructive, but try to think while you're doing this – how would you have played differently and why. What are your underlying motivations and assumptions, and are they helpful? This latter part is the most difficult. Chess improvement is a very personal, deeply psychological matter and the players themselves will often know deep down what they need to do to improve, but if and only if they are honest with themselves.

Metaphysicists have suggested that chess is a 'medieval computer simulacrum, a magical model of the world' (or of time) in which the various forces confront one another. Or an image of life, your opponent representing the tyranny of the outside world. What do you think about these opinions?
I'd like to meet that metaphysicist and ask him what on earth he's talking about!
As far as I know there was nothing resembling computers in medieval times and the vaguest concepts of computation were probably in their infancy. I guess by 'medieval' they just mean primitive, inchoate, ponderous, passive or something similarly related. However, even though there are undoubtedly parallels between chess and life, to speak of a 'simulacrum' in this context is going too far.

Chess is too abstract to be a viable simulacrum, but we can, perhaps, see chess as a model of life in more ways than one. For instance, it tends to have a beginning (youth), a middle (career/family) and an end (old age), it has an essentially agonistic character (just as in life, we are compelled to make difficult decisions), it evokes a variety of emotions and stories can be told through the moves. Even so, life is a much richer tapestry and there is much in life which cannot be found in chess, even on a plausible metaphorical level (sensory pleasures, ethnicity, nose-rings, natural beauty, foreign languages, coriander, underwear, windmills) *(windmills, hmmm!)* for them to be compared in this strong sense.

It might be a model of time in that we speak of 'moments' during games, we talk of a move having a history and we see events unfold in time over the board – the game somehow 'moves' through time and we observe this movement. We also know that just as we must die, the game must end, so there is some natural angst associated with both chess and life. But again, the parallel is not very tidy because chess games can be timeless in a way life can never be. Styles of play do change, but if you show me a random set of games and ask me when and where they are played, I would be struggling in a way I might not if you show me some photographs of events in real life. I would make mistakes of course, but at least *(with the photographs)* I'd have something tangible to go on.

As for the opponent as the tyranny of the outside world, it doesn't seem like a very enlightened view of the game or of the world. Firstly, because we often know and like our opponents and can't deceive ourselves in this way and, secondly, it implies a fairly defeatist view about the outside world, as if it were by definition something hostile to be combated and overcome. If you see the world as essentially benevolent and your opponent as a fellow human, then I believe in the long-term you'll be a much happier person.

What would be your definition of chess?
In terms of a definition, I was quite fond of David Norwood's characterisation for a while – that 'Chess is art with truth' – but then someone suggested that maybe all art is truth (or none of it is) and I was put back out to sea. I've never scratched too deeply for a final definition and I'm not sure it is wise to do so. I don't see why there should be a single definition to capture such an extraordinary phenomenon. So *what* chess is I don't know, but *that* it is I am very glad.

What are you afraid of?
Not being true to myself and leaving important things unsaid.

Do the antics of some chess players make John McEnroe look like the model sportsman? What's going wrong and what role has FIDE played in the disarray in which the chess world currently finds itself?
It is regrettable that the chess world breeds some anti-social behaviour. Perhaps some aspects of the game do lend themselves to character traits like narcissism and competitiveness, but I guess this comes with the territory. I certainly don't think it's a problem that can be tackled at an institutional level.

I don't know much about FIDE and I certainly prefer not to get involved in blaming anyone. There are very few international organisations which run smoothly at all times and I'm not sure the current disarray extends beyond the lack of a clear

World Champion and an enigmatic president with a few radical but eminently reversible ideas.

How can we successfully market chess to a dubious world? Even when the House of Commons debated chess as a sport, the words anorak and nerd were used. How are we to overcome such prejudice?

Do you mean the world is dubious, or that the world thinks chess is dubious?! It's a useful ambiguity because the two go hand in hand. I think the general educational and cultural focus has to change before large numbers of people begin to see the value in a game like chess. The main reason for this is that its value is not immediate; the long-term benefits are hard to quantify, and all attempts to simplify and accelerate chess are double-edged because they undermine the depth and complexity of the game while trying to celebrate it.

It takes some patience to appreciate chess, and this is not as fashionable a virtue as it used to be! Chess could also be called an 'elitist' activity, not in the sense of being unduly or unfairly exclusive, but just as opposed to readily accessible and 'popular'. Let's face it, it's a difficult game and it consumes a lot of time. Perhaps we shouldn't try too hard to market the game as a popular pursuit. Those who love chess tend to love it deeply precisely because of its depth. Much of the game's charm is lost if we simplify or dilute it, and this may not be a price worth paying for making chess more popular. It's a graceful game which waits to be discovered. It's not in its nature to vaunt itself, and it rewards the patience of those who seek it out.

Moreover, efforts to make chess look more 'sexy' and alluring are largely in vain. People won't buy it in the current cultural climate, when there are so many other things to capture their attention. We all know that it can't compete with something like football when it comes to popular appeal, because the thrills it provides, although perhaps more deeply satisfying and personally felt, rarely capture the attention of a crowd.

What we need is a society which supports and respects the activity, but that's not the same as making it popular. The prejudice you mention is endemic, but is not just focused on chess but on anything that doesn't aspire to the (inevitable) straight-jacket worn by popular culture. If something is complex and difficult you can't make instant conversation out of it; you can't trivialise it, and I think that's a good thing.

The future for chess and its improved image lies in education. Not just to continue to bring the game to schools, although that definitely helps, but to have a societal culture where learning is valued and celebrities are celebrated for what they know or can do, rather than because the media inflates them into cultural icons, famous in the end for little more than being famous. When a majority of people start to value ideas and place less emphasis on instant gratification and activities requiring diminutive attention spans, then we may start to get somewhere with popularising chess, but these long-term cultural changes are of course largely out of chess players' hands.

In so far as we can do anything immediately useful, we should raise awareness of the emotional and psychological elements of chess, whilst continuing to promote its cognitive benefits. People will only be engrossed in activities that they can relate to and chess is unusual in that you can only be a spectator while being a participant, in other words watching a game is only interesting if you know what is going on. Most people can't relate to '♘g5 attacks the vulnerable f7-square' but they can relate to 'he won't like that, his soft under-belly is under *(heavy)* fire' – but even that wears thin after a while if you can't generate ideas about the game by yourself.

We have made huge technological advancements. Did the Deep Blue victory signify an end to human superiority, or has this event been over-hyped?

The Deep Blue victory was sad and perhaps unnecessary. We all know that Kasparov wasn't at his best, but perhaps it was just a matter of time in any case. I spoke with Joel Benjamin who worked for Deep Blue and he reckoned that it was at least 2650 in general. There's no reason in principle why it couldn't climb another 200 points in due course.

However, this scare-mongering about the end of human superiority is absolute nonsense, or it at least applies to a very limited domain. If I play the computer and it starts to beat me, I still have many advantages over it:

a) I know I'm playing chess, and am aware of the experience.

b) I can talk about the game and play around with my thoughts.

c) If I get really irritated, I can unplug the computer (or stamp on it).

Basically I can 'jump out of the system' in a way that the computer can't. Of course, computers compute better than humans, but our superiority comes from the fact that the computers are much more dependent on us than we are on them; at least for now!

What do you consider to be your best game?

It's hard to take these things out of context; sometimes you are very proud of a game and buzz for a week, even if it turns out to be pretty lousy on objective analysis. Moreover, some great games are spoiled by a mistake near the end. At the moment, I'd probably choose Wells-Rowson, Canadian Open 2000, because I had to beat a strong Grandmaster and good friend in the last round with Black and played very positively from start to finish.

Wells-Rowson
Canadian Open 2000
Queen Pawn Opening

1 d4 d6 2 ♘f3 ♗g4 3 e4 ♘f6 4

♗d3

This was the last round and Peter Wells knew that a draw would guarantee him a share of first place. Although a win would score outright first, there is a great temptation in such circumstances to play safe. After all, Rowson had to win in order to catch the leaders and so would probably have to take some risks to win. 4 ♘c3 is the main line and gives White the dangerous plan of kingside expansion after 4...e6 5 h3 ♗h5 6 ♕e2, with g2-g4 to follow.

4...e6 5 h3 ♗h5 6 0-0 d5

Black's main idea in such positions, setting up a French pawn structure but with the light-squared bishop outside the pawn chain. In the French White often wants to expand in the centre with e4-e5, but here, with the knight on f3 pinned, this leaves White vulnerable to a quick counterattack with ...c7-c5, ...♘c6 and ...♕b6. Not surprisingly, Wells avoids this.

7 ♘bd2 ♗e7 8 c3 0-0 9 exd5 exd5

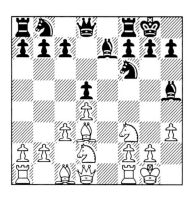

9...♘xd5 is perfectly plausible, but Rowson's idea is to set up an active IQP position.

10 ♖e1 c5!

Black must act before White is able to manoeuvre his knight to g3, with a strong position.

11 dxc5

Now there is no time for 11 ♘f1 because after 11...cxd4 12 cxd4 ♘c6 13 ♗e3 ♕b6 White is under pressure.

11...♗xc5 12 ♘b3 ♗b6

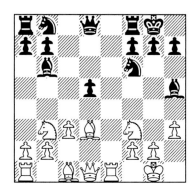

It is well known that the best way of dealing with an isolated queen's pawn is to blockade it and combine this with a kingside fianchetto. In this particular situation White is in no position to successfully implement either plan, which leaves Black very comfortable.

13 ♗g5

The attempt to trade pieces and blockade d4 with 13 ♗e3 does not solve White's problems: 13...♘c6 14 ♗xb6 ♕xb6, when White has considerable difficulty co-ordinating and will find ...♖fe8 awkward to meet. However, after 15 ♗e2 ♖fe8 16 ♘fd4 ♘xd4 17 cxd4 ♗xe2 18 ♖xe2 Black should not be able to win against accurate defence.

The radical 15 g4 leaves White's kingside critically weakened, 15...♗g6 16 ♗xg6 hxg6 17 ♘fd4 a5 seeing White's structural concessions coming back to haunt him.

13...h6 14 ♗h4

White can win a pawn with 14 ♗xf6 ♕xf6 15 g4 ♗g6 16 ♗xg6 ♕xg6 17 ♕xd5 but it is easy to see why Wells rejected this, as after 17...♘c6 Black is very active and White's kingside is vulnerable. Not an ideal situation when a draw is sufficient.

14...♘c6 15 ♗f5 g5

Ironically Rowson can justify this kingside thrust, thanks to the extra space generally afforded the player with the IQP.

16 ♗g3 ♘e4!

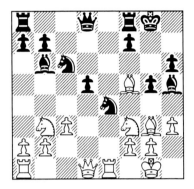

The key move! The weaknesses on g3 and f3 oblige White to accept this positional pawn sacrifice, but Jonathan has foreseen that he will get more than enough compensation.

17 ♗xe4 dxe4 18 ♖xe4 f5

Although it appears that Black is resorting to desperation on the kingside the master plan is to lock White's dark-squared bishop out of the game.

19 ♖e6 ♕xd1+ 20 ♖xd1 f4 21 ♗h2

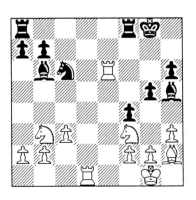

21...♖ad8!

Our Scottish hero's treatment of the position is both admirable and instructive. Most players would rush to play ...♗xf3 here to forever entomb the bishop on h2, but Rowson correctly judges that with the vulnerability of his opponent's back rank it is more important not to give White's king breathing space.

22 ♖xd8

Now Black gets what he wants. The alternative is unattractive but perhaps White should have keep some control of his back rank with 22 ♖de1, although Rowson's advantage is undeniable after 22...♗xf3 23 gxf3 ♔g7.

22...♖xd8 23 ♘fd2

The other knight retreat does not help because Black is able to restore material parity while maintaining his grip on the kingside after 23 ♘bd2 ♗f7 24 ♖e1 (24 ♖xh6 ♔g7 traps the rook) 24...♗xa2 etc.

23...♗f7 24 ♖e2 ♗c4!

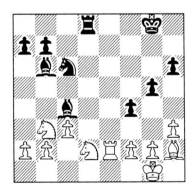

Black's every move creates a threat and he is effectively a piece up.

25 ♖e1 ♘e5!

Turning the screw. It is important to continue making threats, thus denying

White the time to break with g2-g3.

26 ♘xc4

26 ♖xe5 ♗xb3 is quite unpleasant for White.

26...♘xc4 27 ♔f1

There is still no time for 27 g3 as 27...♘d2 threatens either a decisive check on f3 or an infiltration on the seventh rank.

27...♘xb2

Rowson has regained his pawn so now is a good time to take stock of the position. With Black's pieces so active and White's bishop still entombed, Black is simply winning.

28 g3 f3

Fixing yet another weakness on f2.

29 g4

Finally the bishop has gained some air, but this is far too late to save the game.

29...♗xf2!

The simplest way of converting Black's advantage. Jonathan exploits the h2-bishop's awkward placement in order to organise a decisive infiltration on the seventh rank.

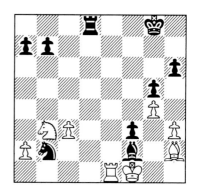

30 ♔xf2 ♘d3+ 31 ♔f1 ♘xe1 32 ♔xe1 ♖e8+ 33 ♔f1 ♖e2 34 ♗g3

The bishop is finally free, but nothing can save the game now.

34...♖xa2 35 ♘d4 a5

Black had doubtless seen this plan when making his 29th move. The a-pawn will cost White a piece.

36 ♘xf3 a4 0-1

A positional masterpiece by Scotland's youngest grandmaster, in which he cleverly kept control of the position at all times. Peter Wells may have lost on time at this point, but the game is winning for Jonathan.

What do you think was the best game ever played?

Again, I don't like this word 'best' much, because there are so many good ones, but probably Karpov-Kasparov, Game 16 of the 1985 World Championship match, with 8...d5 in the Taimanov Sicilian. This is an extremely deep game, with lots of hidden ideas and prophylactic thinking. When you read Kasparov's notes to this game you find it hard to imagine there ever being a stronger human chess player.

Karpov-Kasparov
World Ch. 1985 (Game 16)
Sicilian Defence

1 e4 c5 2 ♘f3 e6 3 d4 cxd4 4 ♘xd4 ♘c6 5 ♘b5

This is White's most direct attempt to take advantage of the Taimanov move order. The knight threatens to hop into d6 and this gives White the opportunity to set up the famous Maroczy bind with his next move.

5...d6 6 c4

White's pawns have a cramping effect, making it difficult for Black to break out beyond his third rank.

6...♘f6 7 ♘1c3 a6

Already the first drawback of White's position is revealed. Only by retreating to a less desirable square can White avoid an exchange that would help Black.

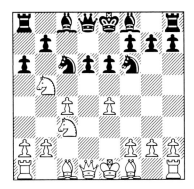

8 ♘a3

The main line. 8 ♘d4 allows a timely ...♘xd4 followed by ...♗d7-c6.

8...d5

Certainly Black's most ambitious move. Typically, Kasparov prefers dynamism to patient manoeuvring. In his own words 'As a rule, such activity in the opening on the part of Black is strategically unfounded, but if one thinks about it, the transfer of the knight from g1 to a3 can hardly be considered an asset for White!'

It is perfectly plausible for Black to play 8...♗e7, with the idea of setting up a 'hedgehog' formation. Black will develop peaceably with ...b7-b6, ...♗b7, ...0-0 and ...♕c7, followed by manoeuvring mostly on the first three ranks, before breaking with a timely ...b6-b5 or ...d6-d5.

9 cxd5 exd5 10 exd5 ♘b4 11 ♗e2

White has other moves but this is still considered to be the critical try here.

11...♗c5

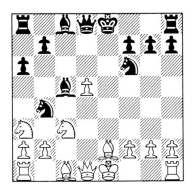

Kasparov goes for maximum piece activity before attempting to regain his pawn. With the benefit of hindsight we can say that this move is over-ambitious, and Black should take the pawn immediately with 11...♘fxd5.

12 0-0

Karpov fails to find the most incisive reply and the danger passes for Black. To his credit, one year later, against Van der Wiel in Brussels 1986, Karpov dismissed Black's set-up with 12 ♗e3, when after 12...♗xe3 13 ♕a4+ ♘d7 14 ♕xb4 ♗c5 15 ♕e4+ ♔f8 16 0-0 b5 17 ♘c2 White had a clear advantage. 13...♗d7 14 ♕xb4 and 13...b5 14 ♕xb4 also leave White with a safe extra pawn.

12...0-0 13 ♗f3 ♗f5

With Karpov missing his best chance Kasparov activates his remaining pieces with gusto.

14 ♗g5 ♖e8 15 ♕d2 b5

Sensibly limiting the possibilities of the poorly placed knight on a3. Unfortunately for Karpov his light-squared weaknesses will not go away.

16 ♖ad1 ♘d3

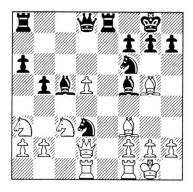

The knight reaches an absolutely awesome position, which if it can be maintained will dictate the course of the game.

17 ♘ab1

17 d6 is White's best chance to meet Black's growing initiative. Then 17...♕xd6 (17...♖a7 18 ♗e2 ♘e5 19 ♘d5 hands the initiative over to White) 18 ♗xa8 ♖xa8 gives Black's very active pieces compensation for the sacrificed exchange, but at least here White has some material to show for his passivity.

17...h6 18 ♗h4 b4!

Black continues to force the pace, driving White's pieces to inferior squares.

19 ♘a4

19 ♘e2 is certainly stronger, but Karpov's slip in the game is entirely understandable considering the intense pressure (at this level it is supposed to be White who presses for the advantage out of the opening). After 19...g5 20 ♗xg5 (20 ♗g3 g4) 20...♘xf2 21 ♖xf2 ♗xf2+ 22 ♔xf2 hxg5 23 ♕xg5+ ♗g6 24 ♘d2 White can hope to save the game.

19...♗d6

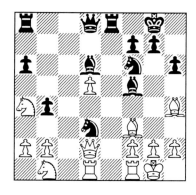

Black begins to assume total control of the position. The extra white pawn is meaningless as Karpov's pieces lack even a hint of harmony. According to Kasparov he had prepared this position in advance. If this is true it shows why Kasparov's home analysis is so feared, as White's major pieces are completely paralysed.

20 ♗g3 ♖c8 21 b3 g5!

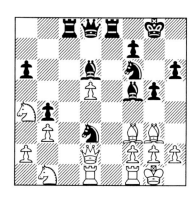

The fact that Black can get away with weakening his kingside like this is a clear sign of his dominance. White is in no position to take advantage of it and must watch out for the arrival of a knight on f4 or the ...g5-g4 thrust.

22 ♗xd6

There is no time to try and get one of

the knights back into play as 22 ♘b2 loses to 22...♘xb2 23 ♕xb2 g4 24 ♗e2 ♖c2. Kasparov gives 22 h4 as White's best chance, although weakening his own king position is hardly Karpov's style. Moreover it is not enough to save the game, as Black has 22...♘f4, again introducing the threat of ...♖c2 and forcing White into 23 hxg5 hxg5 24 ♗xf4 ♗xf4 25 ♕xb4 ♗d6 26 ♕d2 g4 27 ♗e2 ♘h5, after which Black has a decisive attack in view of the twin threats of ...♖c2 and ...♕h4.

22...♕xd6 23 g3 ♘d7!

A multi-purpose move. White has to watch out for possibilities of ...♘e5 and the queen invading his kingside.

24 ♗g2

Karpov still has no time to remove the irritating knight from d3, as Kasparov has prepared a diabolical trap: 24 ♘b2 ♕f6 25 ♘xd3 ♗xd3 26 ♕xd3 ♘e5

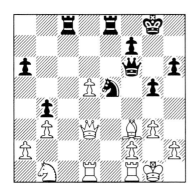

24...♕f6

Ruling out the ♘b2 defence once and for all and effectively sealing White's fate as he cannot co-ordinate his position with the knights so badly out of play.

25 a3

White is in a terrible bind and can hardly move a piece, and this attempt to break out is easily parried.

25...a5 26 axb4 axb4 27 ♕a2 ♗g6

Beginning to build pressure on the f-file.

28 d6

Karpov still cannot use his knights, as 28 ♘d2 is well met by the pin 28...♖e2.

28...g4

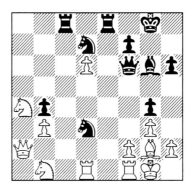

The d-pawn is going nowhere so Black carries on with his kingside plans.

29 ♕d2

Unable to improve his situation, Karpov is reduced to one move threats.

29...♔g7 30 f3

If White does not weaken his kingside in this manner Black has the strong plan of marching the h-pawn up the board.

30...♕xd6

With White weakening his kingside it is time to remove the pawn, thus freeing the blockading knight for an important role in the coming attack.

31 fxg4 ♕d4+ 32 ♔h1 ♘f6

The knight is on a 'search and destroy' mission. The f2-square is White's prominent weakness and Black is ideally placed to exploit this.

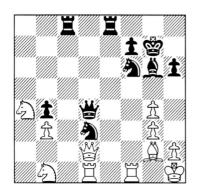

33 ♖f4

Now Karpov's position heads rapidly downhill, but there is no adequate defence, e.g. 33 h3 ♖e3 34 ♔h2 ♘e4 35 ♖f4 ♘xd2 36 ♖xd4 ♘xb3.

33...♘e4

A bone crusher! White cannot deal with the multiple threats.

34 ♕xd3

34 ♗xe4 is equally hopeless in view of 34...♗xe4+ 35 ♖xe4 ♕xe4+ 36 ♔g1 ♘e5, and Black will crash through on f3 and/or c2.

34...♘f2+ 35 ♖xf2 ♗xd3 36 ♖fd2 ♕e3!

Kasparov does not rest on his laurels

and moves in for the kill as swiftly as possible.

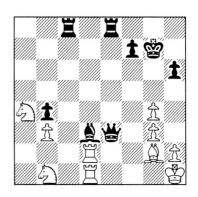

37 ♖xd3 ♖c1 38 ♘b2

One of the errant knights finally finds a way back into the game, just in time to see the finish.

38 ♖xe3 ♖xd1+ 39 ♗f1 ♖xe3 wins easily for Black.

38...♕f2 39 ♘d2 ♖xd1+ 40 ♘xd1 ♖e1+ 0-1

Karpov was strangled in a manner he would have truly admired, had he not been on the wrong side. A masterpiece that, at the time, Kasparov considered his greatest creative achievement.

What would be your pearl of wisdom to the chess-playing world?

Affirm your mistakes; don't deny them. Try to appreciate them and learn from them because they are inevitable. Observe yourself carefully before you play and enjoy the experience of playing.

And, of course, buy my books!

CONCLUSION

How were the interviews conducted?

Michael Adams and Yasser Seirawan were done face to face. Nigel Short, Julian Hodgson and Joel Lautier were done by telephone, while Alexander Khalifman, Sofia Polgar and Jonathan Rowson were done via email. Finally, Emil Sutovsky's interview was a combination of telephone conversations and email.

Can we reach any conclusions about the secrets of the Grandmaster mind?

Well, I hope that you feel suitably enlightened, but I fear that we can, sadly, reach very few conclusions, except on the one point about which everyone agrees – hard work is the key. Work, work and more work. What I will also say is that there are many more Grandmasters in the world with extraordinary amounts of knowledge to impart. I heartily welcome your feedback on this book, for if I am to produce another collection of Grandmaster interviews I will need further lines of questioning. Please send all comments and/or suggestions to me via the publisher's address or website. For those of you who feel the need for more guidance than the Grandmasters offered in these pages I would like to leave you with this small collection of entertaining, poignant and worthwhile chess pearls of wisdom.

Chess is...

Life – Bobby Fischer

Mental torture – Garry Kasparov

Everything: art, science and sport – Anatoly Karpov

A fairy tale of 1001 blunders – Savielly Tartakower

99 percent tactics – Teichmann

99 percent calculation – Soltis

Now for some sensible advice:

When you see a good move, wait and look for a better one – Emanuel Lasker

All that matters on the chessboard is good moves – Bobby Fischer

A good chess player is always lucky – Capablanca

There are two types of sacrifices: correct ones and mine – Tal

The pin is mightier than the sword – Reinfeld

Even a poor plan is better than no plan at all – Mikhail Chigorin

The hardest thing to win is a won game – Tarrasch

The tactician knows what to do when there is something to do, whereas the strategian knows what to do when there is nothing to do – Gerald Abrahams

Half the variations which are calculated in a tournament game turn out to be completely superfluous. Unfortunately, no one knows in advance which half – Jan Timman

The Passed Pawn is a criminal, who should be kept under lock and key. Mild measures, such as police surveillance, are not sufficient – Nimzowitsch

No price is too great for the scalp of the enemy king – Koblentz

Life is too short for chess – Byron (he must have just lost a horrible game!)

All the following are from Tartakower, who obviously spent as much time on his proverbs as he did his chess

The blunders are all there on the board, waiting to be made.

The winner of the game is the player who makes the next-to-last mistake.

It's always better to sacrifice your opponent's men.

A chess game is divided into three stages: the first, when you hope you have the advantage, the second, when believe you have an advantage, and the third... when you know you are going to lose!

Finally, my absolute favourite (remember this, and know that every word is true):

Every chess master was once a beginner – Chernev